LIFE COMPASS

Keys To Discovering Your Purpose
and Executing Your Life Orderly

Dr. Chilungamo Khuwi
Foreword by: Assoc. Prof. Chiwoza
Bandawe (Clinical Psychologist
- University of Malawi)

Lighted Insight Publishing House

ISBN-13: 9789996099021

Cover design by: Dr. Azariah Mosiwa
Printed in Malawi

CONTENTS

FOREWORD

You hold in your hands a life resource which, if read and applied, will guarantee you a unique, productive and joyful life. The principles outlined in this book are universal laws of life which most people are not exposed to, yet these laws are in operation all the time and determine the outcomes of our lives. Chilungamo Khuwi has systematically unpacked some of these laws to help us better manage, plan and live purposeful lives. He shares some of his own experiences in an applied and practical manner. Many have grown up and gone through the stages of life without this crucial knowledge. In many ways, you are blessed to have this knowledge come to you right now.

The adage, "If you fail to plan, you plan to fail" by Benjamin Franklin comes alive in this ground-breaking book. Beginning with the core concept of identity, Chilungamo takes you on a reflective journey that forces you to pause and think along each step of the way. He then marries your identity to the concept of purpose, your life isn't just there for fun, there is a purpose to it, and you need to understand and build your decisions around what that is. Our lives are part of a bigger design and the book addresses spirituality and how we can connect with God through meditation.

Our character defines us and determines the personality that outputs from us. This is beautifully unpacked in this book.

The book takes on a practical and applied approach addressing leadership, finances and relationships all with real examples from Chilungamo's life. You will gain the greatest value from this book by continuously applying what you read to your own life. It is a book that will jump-start your life from living other people's visions for you to taking back responsibility and ownership for the outcome of your life. As you read, pause and reflect. We know that reflection is an important aspect of mental wellbeing. This book promotes many aspects of your wellbeing. It is your companion for a successful and God honouring life.

St. Irenaeus is reported to have said: "The glory of God is man fully alive". In other words, when you come fully alive, you live the purpose for which God created you, you contribute to the growth and development of humanity, then God is glorified. With this book, you are set on the course for coming fully alive, alive to your life mission, fulfilled relationships and the manifestation of the application of the universal laws of life you will be expose to. The world needs alive people. Come alive! Your time has come!

Dr Chiwoza Bandawe,
Clinical Psychologist, University of Malawi

INTRODUCTION

"And he said to them, "Take care, and be on your guard against all covetousness, for one's life does not consist in the abundance of his possessions." **Luke 12:15**

"There is one quality one must possess to win, and that is the definiteness of purpose, the knowledge of what one wants and the burning desire to achieve it." **Napoleon Hill**

When you wake up every day, you are always walking around and doing all sorts of things. As you walk around, you walk into the future as you leave the present into the past. You get tired, you rest and sleep ready to continue your walk to the future when you wake up again. Therefore, living your life is a journey to the future, and you are the vehicle that carries yourself on the journey to your future.

Your life (who you are as a human being) is a development project. Just like every other development project, your life should have an end picture (blueprint) which you are aiming for. Because life is a journey to the future, it means there should be a destination (destiny) you are locked on. To get to that destination, your life should be developed into a proper vehicle (the end picture or tool) that is fit to carry out the needed assignments and go through the challenges along the way.

Having that in mind, that vehicle should be made with the right materials, with the right characteristics, and having the right shape to be on the road to your destination. In other words, you need to develop into a person (the vehicle or tool), with the right features, that is fit to take you to your destiny.

For you to decide the kind of vehicle (person) needed to take you to your destination you first should know what that destination is. The destination determines the means, the design and characteristics of the materials to be used in building that vehicle according to the challenges anticipated along the journey to your destiny.

I've come to realize that most people's lives lack direction primarily due to ignorance of their destination. People don't know what they should be chasing, or what they should be building on, therefore they don't know or recognize the resources they need to build their lives with and how to use them. Most people are not intentional about their lives in the way they make their decisions because they don't have a right basis when it comes to decision making.

Life was or is meant to be simple and straight forward only we understand what it should be about. Do you agree with that? There is a way how life is ideally meant to be lived. There are essential pillars that make up a healthy and fulfilled life which everyone must observe and follow.

There is a way how life is meant to be built from the ground up. A lot of times we live unfulfilled empty lives. We define our lives by the things that can be lost or taken away from us. Once removed our foundations become shaky. We needed to focus on things that establish us and help us handle the external forces that come from pursuing secondary things. The hidden secret which most people don't realize is that once you get to understand and master the primary things first, it becomes easier to gain secondary things.

You are not the things you possess, accumulate or do outside of your body. You are everything intangible that is within you – purpose, knowledge, character, and spirituality and belief system. Life boils down to who you are and what you carry within you wherever you go.

Life is a personal journey which is completely tailored to you. There is no reason for you to compare yourself to anyone else because you are building different things. As much as you may compete with others for resources and opportunities, you can never and should never compare your structure to anyone. You don't do what others are doing that you shouldn't be

doing just to get applauded.
What is right for them usually is not right for you since you have different purposes. The vision and the goals you have in life should be tailored to your purpose.

Your life needs a purpose, a vision, goal setting, resources to build that vision into reality and make it effective, network with other purposes and visions around you to have a greater impact on the world.

If indeed your life as a human being is a project what's your blueprint? Now that you know that life is a journey to the future, and you are serious to get to your destination, can you afford to continue without a LIFE COMPASS? Have you gotten yours already? Have you figured it out?

Let's be together as I will be unfolding where I believe people could be missing it in life, why people have a midlife crisis and why they regret on their deathbed. I believe they regret because of misplaced priorities, and all because they lack a LIFE COMPASS.

This book will help you realize where, why and how you should spend your time, mind, energy and resources as you pursue a happy, successful, productive, fulfilling and meaningful life that you will never regret to have lived.

PREFACE

This is the first book in the Growth and Development Series. These books are aimed at building you from the ground up with the hopes of attaining a meaning and successful life. I believe life should be developed in stages. I believe life should be governed by the principles of life. Every building needs a foundation, and every foundation needs structure. What about you?

The first twenty years of my life had me spiralling. I had no sense of real direction. My mentor Dr Cornelius Huwa came in and helped me to see life in a new light. This shaped me (and continues to) and set up the necessary building blocks for an intentional and purposeful life. I have since seen the rise and build of my life all-round and sustainably.

In this series, I will share with you the principles of greatness. It doesn't matter where you are or how broken your life is. To start with keen consistent diligence is key. Thorough knowledge of the right principles and adherence to proper guidance, we can all become successful, fulfilled and influential. The difference between successful and unsuccessful people is in whether they do or don't according to the knowledge or exposure they have or lack thereof.

This series is not exactly about how to do specific practices per se but rather about principles that should help to bring your life into perspective and balance so that you operate as one machine going in one direction. It's about showing you how to bring the world around you in subjection to your purpose as you influence the world around you through that purpose.

THEME ONE:

BASIC AREAS OF LIFE

"But seek first the kingdom of God and his righteousness, and all these things will be added to you." **Matthews 6:33**

"Put first things first and second things are thrown in. Put second things first and you lose both first and second things." **– C.S Lewis**

⚘ FIRST THINGS FIRST

Chapter One

Every person's life is made up of primary and secondary things. Primary things are what makeup who you are and why you do certain things (motives or intents). That which is secondary is birthed from the primary; the things that you do and how you do them.

The entirety of your being (all that encompasses you) often dictates the ingredients of the primary. In other words, you are the primary! It is everything about you. They are the substance or the particles that make up who you are, your essence. These are things that define you and can't be separated from you. Such things include identity, spirituality, purpose, and character. Though the primary things are the essence of who you are, the positive aspects do not always come automatically. Though they are within reach they are things which we normally should be conscious and intentional about if we want to develop them. Good character doesn't come just like that, one needs to deliberately develop just as discovering one's purpose, learning, spirituality and leadership. All these need efforts though they are part of who we are.

As mentioned before, secondary things are things that you do and how you do them. Things like finance, career, friendships, marriage, etc. are all secondary things because they are not directly part of who you are.

Let me break it to you that personality, just as habits, is part of secondary things because they are not who you are but rather emanate from who you are. Who you are, determines how you behave or the way you do certain things? You can never fake who you truly are. You can, however, fake how you behave. Even though you can fool people about who you are through your personality, you know who you are (your intentions) at the core. People have resorted to quick-fix their lives through developing personality traits to convince people or win people over, the dos and don'ts, 'how-tos, etc.

There is a basic structure of life, a minimum composition of areas which every human being should be good at to have a functional life. This is where you need to start building your life from, and this same principle applies to businesses, institutions and machines. This basic structure enables things to deliver on their minimum expectations. The rest of the things are there for extra value, to beautify or to spice up things one way or another. For example, paint on a car is not mainly applied for the car performance rather the outlook and prevention of rust which adds more beauty, durability of the wood hence value to be sold at a higher price..

Every primary thing in your life is an essential need because it's the foundation or forms the skeleton for your life. If primary things are not in place then your success, if you manage to attain it at all, is temporary. Among the secondary things, there are also essential areas that even though they are outside of us, we still need to master them for effective living.

Primary things are things that you should seek out to work on first and foremost. They have great bearing on your secondary things. It's easy to attain secondary things when you have primary things figured out but very hard to work on primary things when you have secondary things. Though not impossible, it can be quite the challenge to work on primary areas which have survived years of misinformed ideas when the secondary structures (relationships, money management) have already been erected. Some secondary structures are built from the wrong premise. Though hard, it is not impossible.

People are busy focusing on secondary things that are not essential such as career, possession of material things, etc, which just add extra value, without first sorting out the essential needs of life. Value is added to something that's already there. It's like having a beautiful car hood without an engine and you are busy perfecting it. You can't drive it no matter how beautiful you make it. You need to have something operational which you should add value to; you need to have the basics of your life going before you think of jumping into certain things in life. Because of such disorder, people end up living chaotic lives and wonder why their lives are all over the place and nothing to show for their efforts over time.

The same thing goes to organizations and businesses which need basic or essential things in place for them to run effectively and last, the rest are just additional elements. Things like purpose, mission, essential workers or departments, core values and governing principles, funding are essential to the business.

I believe every individual should be good at these essential areas no matter who they are, what they do or don't, whether single or married, white or black; these basic areas are cross-cutting. Remember essential doesn't only mean primary areas but all primary areas are automatically essential. These essential areas in a human life include purpose, vision, mission, identity, character, spirituality, leadership, finance and relationship. We are involved in all these areas one way or another, both at individual and group level.

Let me order these things according to their importance in the structure: the purpose is the why to your life (or why something exists). Spirituality, Moral Fortitude (good character) and personal leadership are the foundation by which you stand (or fall). Money making and relationship management are but the supporting pillars that ensure sturdiness and form.

EVERYTHING EXISTS WITH AND FOR A PURPOSE

Chapter Two

"The greatest tragedy in life is not death, but life without a purpose." **Dr Myles Munroe**

In the "Purpose Driven Life" book by Rick Warren, he posed a question that says, "What on Earth am I here for?" This might sound very basic but really what are you here on earth for? Most of the time, we think we have it all figured out but when we lie back on our beds, close our eyes and search deep within ourselves, we realize that perhaps we have not figured it out yet. But once you truly find your core purpose on this earth then I believe you have taken the first step to your fulfilment and executing your life orderly as one machine to the future with a guarantee of no regrets.

Even though a car may have different parts, and each one serving its purpose, when you put them and their purposes together you have a much bigger machine – the car. If you look around, you will realize that there is something common about life, from the smallest organism to the biggest of galaxies; everything is interlinked with each one performing a certain purpose (and in the end all serving a greater purpose).

Look at the world: animals need oxygen and food from plants, and we breathe out carbon dioxide and animal wastes are used by the plants for food. Bees feed on pollen to make honey that humans and other animals feed on, yet they help with pollination of flowers in the process which produces seeds in plants.

Your body is a system of systems. Each system has its purpose or function which it serves to other systems and self in the body and affects the function of other systems within the same body. Together they form you and all your function and abilities as a human being that affects your surroundings. Take note that these systems, in your body, are also made up of organs that also have their unique purpose or function to their respective systems.

We have the respiratory system (breathing; oxygen uptake into the body and carbon dioxide release – Nose, trachea (windpipe) and lungs), cardiovascular system (Food, oxygen, immunity supply, chemical waste transportation from to the whole body - heart, blood and blood vessels), Gastrointestinal system (Nutrition - month, oesophagus, stomach and intestines), neurology (Command and action centre; Sensation and reaction - Brain, spinal cord and nerves), Genitourinary system (Controls water, salts and chemical levels in the body - Kidneys, ureters, bladder, urethra) among others.

All these depend on each other for function and

effectiveness. No system can function long enough without oxygen, food, proper levels of water, salts and chemicals, and without proper control to do so. Though they are unique in their functions, they are affected by the function of the other.

The heart pumps blood that carries oxygen and food to the bones and muscles and in turn, the muscles and bones support and protect the heart and other delicate organs and carry the whole body to places. The brain tells the body what to do and how to do it and the rest of the body follows the orders. It's not the brain that executes, all it does is to receive data from the rest of the organs, process it and send back commands for the rest of the systems in the body to act upon.

Let me take you to another angle, look at organizations, businesses and governments. These are all systems made up of departments or sections and each one serves its purpose and they operate as one machine when their effects are brought together. Usually, you find individuals within departments serving their specific purposes or roles. If one individual is not doing their job right, then the department is usually affected.

A dysfunctional marketing, production or sales department sinks the whole business machine. Each of those business departments even though performing a different task yet have a greater effect on the overall performance of the other and the whole institution.

From all these examples, you will realize that at every level there is a system made up of different parts and systems whose purpose or function aids in the function of the other. Together all of them they have even a greater purpose or function. This is how life is or should be at every level including you as an individual or us as a society. Everything that exists has a purpose to meet by design and I believe behind the creation there is an awesome Designer who thought it wise to put interconnected systems that aid each other for sustenance and greater effect upon our societies, nations, continents and whole earth.

If your life is dysfunctional in some areas, I wouldn't call that successful life. As much as other people or you may call it as such, but it is a limited or incomplete success because it is in just one or two departments of your life. Such limited success in a few areas of your life limits your overall effect on earth. You can call it a successful job, career, business, marriage or ministry yes but not successful life. There are systems in your organization (life) that are not firing and until you get them fixed, you, as a machine or organization, are dysfunctional. Those systems will either sink you or hold you back from taking off to make a real impact. People will usually judge you by the areas that are not firing.

From the interconnection and dependency shown above, you should also realize that for a functional world we need not only our unique purpose or function in the society but also support each other. Our functions are not just for us but more so for those around us, for their optimal functioning and maximizing their results.

We should stop trying to be like other people or try to live their lives because they need us to be who we should be for a functional society or nation. We also shouldn't stand in others' way because their success somewhat affects ours, whether we recognize it or not. We shouldn't be blinded by jealousy; their success doesn't mean our failure rather an environment optimized for our function.

⚜ BE FRUITFUL AND MULTIPLY

Chapter Three

"And God blessed them. And God said to them, "Be fruitful and multiply and fill the earth and subdue it and have dominion over the fish of the sea and over the birds of the heavens and over every living thing that moves on the earth." **Genesis 1:28**

When God created man, He commanded him to be fruitful and multiply. It was not only in the filling sense (numbers) but also in productivity. He meant that whatever we are purposed to do, we should do it with all our might and be productive, and multiply in the size of that productivity.

Nonetheless, it doesn't mean that we should be doing everything that comes our way in this life. There is something unique and special for every one of us to be fruitful and multiply in. Not everything good is right for you. The fact that you can do it doesn't mean you should be at it. There is something specific for you that only you can do.

So, what are these things that each one of us needs to focus on and how do we figure them out? This is the million-dollar question that most people don't get to answer for the rest of their earthly lives and that is partly why this book was born. What are your roles and responsibilities here on earth?

As earlier said, there is more to fruitfulness for a man than just procreation. Fruitfulness is productivity. The same goes for multiplication, it is not just an issue of increasing the number of people. It has to do with increasing your production ability. Multiplication also means grooming others to be people of your kind or calibre, people that are focussed and expanding in all that they do.

When you look at a cow, its fruitfulness is not just in bearing the young ones but also in producing milk that people can drink from. It is in producing the manure that plants can benefit from; the meat that people can eat; the hide that shoes can be produced from.

Though a dairy cow may also produce meat, manure and hide, its primary focus is milk production. Therefore, focusing primarily on developing the efficiency of the milk production system should be the ultimate thing. If it had the abilities to enlarge certain parts of the body, then udders would have been the primary focus. Similarly, some cows are solely to produce meat. Though they can produce milk, their goal rests in growing as big as possible; the rest are by-products.

Though various aspects of your life may call for your attention, there is always a specified niche that calls even louder. This is your ultimate purpose in life. For you to determine your area of focus, several things must align to recognize your Eden, the kind of garden in which God placed you in. Not every garden grows the same kind of crops. Not all farming skills apply to all gardens. The 'how' of farming is largely dependent on the crop type, the soil, the climate and the season. My garden's location (environment) is not the same as yours. The skills and knowledge I need and the actions I need to take will differ from yours. Even though principles and practices mirror and share common 'how's', their applicability and contexts may differ.

Even though you can be many things in different places and to different people there is or should be one thing that you will be known by. Even though Mandela was a son, brother, uncle and father to different people, yet to the whole world he was a leader and a freedom fighter. Though he possessed other roles and responsibilities, his legacy remains coined to these two words: freedom fighter.

Despite the multiplicity of the attributes that you possess which are vividly displayed to those around you, there is something or some things about you that are a common denominator. These are often closely tied to your overall purpose. Those with leadership traits often carry such an aura into their daily musings. If you enjoy providing counsel; your workplace, church and school will often be met with surplus opportunities for you to demonstrate the array of quality. Whatever your profession might be, you may find yourself weaving the grand fabric of your personhood through the mundane dealings of your work.

Recently, I listened to the commencement speech by the late Chadwick Boseman – (The King of Wakanda) at Howard University. In his speech, he touched on purpose and he said, *"This day when you have reached the hilltop and you are deciding on next jobs, next steps, careers, further education, you would rather find purpose than a job or career. Purpose crosses disciplines. Purpose is an essential element of you. It is the reason you are on the planet at this particular time in history. Your very existence is wrapped up in the things you are here to fulfil."*

The 'garden' you have been placed in, the inherent desires and talents placed in you by God aid in directing you towards your purpose. Whatever you do in that garden affects everything in and connected to it (people and their environments).

Let it not be mistaken that those without 'talent' (inborn ability) are unable to fortify the necessary tools to enable them to fulfil their God-given purposes. Unlike talent, no one is born with the skill. Skill is wrought. Skill can be learnt to cover for the lacking talents. Some people are born leaders but that doesn't mean that leaders can't be made.

Though we may not all have platforms with thousands of followers, our primary follower is ourselves. We must therefore harness the skills of leadership.

God placed you on this earth to be fruitful and multiply in things that bring peace, order, joy, solutions and the best of others. You need to find out what that is. Why were you born in that continent, country, city, community or family at such a time as this? What things can you do something about, that need sorting for the world to be a better place according to the natural desires and talents embedded in you?

🌿 FRAMING YOUR LIFE

Chapter Four

A wise man once told me that life on earth is meant to be lived to leave a positive mark, that's the whole purpose of life. I believe one of the reasons people hit midlife crisis or deathbed regrets is because they live life without discovering their purpose; they fail to find out where they are meant to leave their mark.

Coming this far, I want to submit to you that the purpose for your life should be the focus or centre of your life. He who created you created you with a purpose and for a purpose. You may be successful in business and the corporate world yet find yourself empty. We often think that our careers are our purpose (and perhaps so). Yet having something to keep you insatiably does not always equate to you living a purposeful and fulfilled life. People can have all that but still hit a wall.

Purpose is something that you can't knock off or retire from. It's the essence of your being. You are miserable without it. If you were to be given $1 billion today, would you still be going to work and be doing what you do? If you wouldn't that tells you your work isn't your purpose but just a means to earn a living. If it was then money wouldn't have to change anything. It shows you that your purpose lies somewhere else where you will probably spend that money on to make an impact.

Careers were introduced to fill the need in our world system – make it a better place. Many people have jobs solely for money generation purposes.

People are often mistakenly making their careers their purpose. In the long run, no matter how much good they have done in their career, for their institutions, they still feel empty and unsatisfied. He that created us placed a unique vacuum that can only be filled by our God-given purpose. You don't define your purpose. You discover it. It's already there.

Everything in your life should revolve around your ultimate purpose. Every decision you make should be in line with it. If I were to pay or reward you, I would do so if and only if first and foremost you have fulfilled what I hired you for. If I ask you to wash my car and you decide to wash my clothes, no matter how clean they can get, I wouldn't commend nor pay you for what you have done.

Your workplace pays you for the purpose or job description they defined for you at work. That job description is a measure of your effectiveness at a workplace, whether you are paid or fired it all depends on

it. Your spouse commends you depending on whether you are fulfilling your roles and responsibility or not as a husband or wife. The same way God rewards our conscience with fulfilment, joy and peace when we fulfil that purpose we were created to accomplish.

Your purpose should determine decisions in every area of your life. What you do in every area should be a means or a tool to advance your purpose. Before you apply for a job or school, get into a relationship, a tool to advance your purpose. Before you apply for a job or school, get into a relationship, business, church, etc. you must first define why. Why that job, why that school, why that lady, why that man and how do they fit in long term, in your purpose? How do they add value to your life? Do they make you better for your purpose or how exactly do they advance your purpose?

Look for a lady who is going in the same direction or would love to and if you are a lady ask the man where he is headed before you say yes. It's never about how rich or poor they are. It's about the direction they are taking and hence the value they will add to your life. Look for friends that are going in the same direction or may add value one way or another. Look for a church and job that will push you in the direction of your purpose. Look for school or a career path that will equip you with knowledge and skills that will advance your purpose. Life is not just about money making and survival. Yes, it's an important bit but not all there is.

So, before you continue, if you don't know what you are here for, sit down and search through your life what you think you can do to add value to those around you which defines you. The rest of the book will be building on that. It will be more meaningful and helpful if you take your time, search and write it down. Most of the time, it gets crystal clear with time, so you will refine it along the way; for now, just have somewhere to start from.

There are two topics in this book that will help you with ideas on how you can figure out what your purpose is and why it is vital for your discovery.

❧ IDENTITY

Chapter Five

"For those whom he foreknew, he also predestined..."
Romans 8:29

Identity is who you are or how you look at yourself as. Every one of us behaves and carries him- or herself according to who we think we are. It's good to search within ourselves who we are because it's until we discover this when we can start to pursue something.

So, your identity is not just about your genetic makeup but more so the tool you should become or the end picture of the person (vehicle) you should develop into that will take you to your destination. Something that people will identify or characterize you by.

If you don't know your purpose in life you can discover it through your identity, and if you don't know your identity you can have an idea if you know what your purpose is. You are a tool to achieve something and what that tool is, is your identity.

The struggle of identity crisis is real and if you didn't struggle with it already, I wouldn't want you to. I faced this problem when I was in my second and third

year of college and I kept on changing my names to fit

the purpose I was feeling deep inside. Since it wasn't clear on what I was supposed to do, every time I got a clearer picture, I changed my name to fit that picture until I finally got the name that best described what my purpose was and hence describes who I am.

It wasn't really about finding the perfect name but rather figuring out who I should be. I was an unstable person till I figured out who I was supposed to be. That's when I surely started building forward.

The piece of the scripture on the previous page is one of my favourites and talks about foreknowing and predestination. Foreknowing is about who you should be - your identity whilst predestination is about what you should do or accomplish – your purpose. If you want to treat the sick, then be a doctor first. If you are to lead, then develop into a leader first. If you are to deal with injustice in the world, then be a tool that naturally not only hates but can also readily deal with the injustice in the world, e.g., a lawyer or a judge but it's not limited to professional qualification.

For the same reason, it took Joseph 13 years from the time he dreamt of leading to the time he led in Egypt. All that time, God made sure he was developed into a leader to meet the challenge. The same way with Jesus, even though He was the Saviour, He still had to develop into the saviour He needed to be to execute the role orderly and to the letter.

Let me also take this opportunity to tell you that there is power in names. Names are not just there for the sake of calling each other but rather they give us identities. They are not only used to identify us but also give us an identity. I used to wonder why I hate injustice till I connected it to my name "Chilungamo" (Justice). This is the reason why Jesus had almost a name for every role He had to play. This is the reason God is so specific with names with the people He worked with because He knows the power of names. Abraham, Sarah, Israel, Jesus among others, carried names that signified their purposes.

In the garden of Eden, Adam didn't just give names to the animals but the characters or behaviours per the meaning of their names. It was more of giving them their identities. Every time people call you by your name, they establish the meaning or character of that name upon you, and you know that words create. That's why the people who are named after certain people end up behaving similar to their namesakes. You keep on calling a child stupid and that is what they end up becoming, stupid! Who you are determines what you do.

You may divert into becoming and behaving in a way you weren't meant to just because your parents gave you a certain name that's holding you back. It is primarily your responsibility to discover who you should be and what you should accomplish in this life and go for it, regardless of the name that your parents gave you. If the name that you have is limiting you, please do change just as a lot of people have. As said earlier, God changed a lot of names of people He worked with for the same reason of marrying the names to their purposes or destinies.

Why Is It Necessary to Figure Out Who You Are Or Should Be?

As earlier said, figuring out your identity is about figuring who you are or should be; the person that you should develop into. Like seeing the "In-shape" you and start hitting the gym to bring that person out.

Figuring out the tool you are or should develop into gives you stability and focus. You know exactly the kind of person you should be developing into and you pursue that. You are not intimidated by what others are developing into because you know they are not you and they aren't taking anything away from who you should be.

Knowing who you should be and developing into that person will get you closer to becoming the tool or the person who is supposed to carry out your purpose. If you want to save people from something you first need to develop into that saviour from deep within your soul. The way you think, behave, speak and act, everything has to ooze the saviour in you. That way it comes out naturally from you to do the saving that's needed to be done.

When you know who you are or should be, you know exactly what you are supposed to do. If you see your-self as a leader you know you should be leading in something or certain people somewhere. If you see yourself as a teacher, you know you should be teaching someone something somewhere.

It also helps you to realize the kind of exposure or education you need. What a freedom fighter needs to learn is different from what a teacher needs to learn about their purposes; they need different knowledge and skills though some things may be common.

How Do You Know Who You Are or Should Be?

Let your purpose guide you into a person you should be because it takes a person of a certain calibre to achieve something naturally. If you were meant to teach people through books then be an author or blogger from inside out, and writing will become you and you will do so naturally. Discover what you should accomplish, and you will know who you should be.

Your natural desires and natural talents also give you an idea of who you are because this also directs you to what your purpose is. Who-you-should-be reveals your potential – what you can do, and what you can do also directs you to who you should be. You can tell what something is and what it is supposed to achieve through knowing its characteristics or properties. Discover those properties and characteristics within you and you will discover who you are or should be.

So, who are you or who should you be in this life?

⚘ WHAT IS PURPOSE?

Chapter Six

Purpose in simplest terms is the job description for your life. It is the thing you are expected to do. The thing that haunts you when you don't do it, when you should have been doing it. It is the impact you owe to the world around you. Imagine that there is someone who will reward you for accomplishing certain things he or she expects you to do. Those things that you are expected to do is your purpose. A purpose meets a need.

So, purpose is the reason for your existence. Something that you were designed specifically to accomplish. There is a reason for your heart's natural desires. There is a reason you lack peace when certain things are being done injustice to. It is something that you can do and are fulfilled. You can work 24/7 without being paid for and without being bored or tired of doing it. It is the one thing you desire to do to make a difference in the world.

If you are a Christian and you read the Bible you will understand why Jesus said His food was to do the will of Him who sent Him and finish His work (John 4:34). He had His fulfilment and joy in teaching and preaching the Gospel of the Kingdom and healing the sick because that was His purpose. He could do it all day, walking around from city to city without complaining about it. Mandela fought without turning back because that was his purpose – to liberate the people of South Africa.

Your purpose for life, just like any organ in the body or part in a machine, is not about serving yourself. The purpose for life is about making a difference to the world around you. It's what you do for others whether you are paid for it or not. You were never put here on earth with talents and skills just to exercise them to yourself. No. It is for the world to benefit as you make it a better home for everyone.

"The purpose of life is not to be happy. It is to be useful, to be honourable, to be compassionate, to have it make some difference that you have lived and lived well." **- Ralph Waldo Emerson**

The purpose is where your legacy is born from. When you build on your purpose so well, you build something that makes a difference in people's lives even when you are long gone. We have Christians today because of something that took place 2020 years ago; all because Jesus knew and invested on his purpose. What a legacy! What will be your legacy?

WHY UNDERSTAND YOUR PURPOSE?

Chapter Seven

"All things are lawful for me, but all things are not expedient: all things are lawful for me, but all things edify not." **1 Corinthians 10:23**

There are several reasons why it is vital to understand one's purpose. As you have seen from the definition, the purpose is key to how you live your life on earth. The following are some of the reasons why you should understand your purpose:

Acts as A LIFE COMPASS

Knowing your life's purpose helps you to have a true north. You know where your destination is, the thing you are trying to achieve in life.

This helps you with planning your life. You make everything about you deliberate because you want everything to add to your journey. You don't jump into things that are taking you away from your destiny because you know where you are going.

You know what education to have or which institutions to work for because they are going in the same direction as you. They are advancing your heart's desire.

What would it benefit you to have a "great" career, spouse, ministry and friends only to realize later that they led you astray from your purpose? Why not sit down now, discover your true north and define and choose everything around you that will push or pull you in the right direction?

Acts as A Reference Point or A Sieve
"It's easy to say "no!" when there's a deeper "yes!" burning inside." **Stephen R. Covey**

Purpose is the backbone of your life. There shouldn't be an area of life that is not in harmony or doesn't feed into your purpose. Your environment should be defined by your purpose.

It holds all things together through the provision of a common direction so that you move forward in one direction without being pulled away by any area of your life. It makes sure your choices in every area are made with respect to it. It helps you focus your energy for a maximum impact on your life.

It determines what values, standards and governing principles to be conceived, birthed and nurtured in your

life. You know the kind of values, standards and principles that will protect and enhance your growth to meeting that purpose.

Run your life purposefully as a business or an organization because your true sense of accomplishment depends on it.

For a minute, look at your life as an institution or an organization you work for or know of, I-TECH, UNICEF, government, Save the Children, Malawi-Liverpool Welcome Trust, College of Medicine, The International Rescue Organisation, Red Cross, a church, bank, you name it. Now, imagine such an organization or institution running without a purpose, mission, goals and objectives. How will they decide which projects to take up or not if they have no specific need to meet? How are they going to define success without a reference point? How would they define whether a potential employee has the necessary qualifications or skills to help their organization move forward or not? How would they measure progress? This tells you how important purpose is.

How do you define the skills you need, the woman or man to date and marry, the resources you need, the type of job you need to be in or business to do, where to spend your money and time, the kind of friends to have and which church to go to? If you don't know your purpose, how then do you define these things? How do you sieve through things to remain with the right ones?

Before I asked my Wife out, I had to first understand what I am here on earth for and who is a better fit to help me get this purpose done. Unsurprisingly when I asked her out, not sure whether I knew what I was doing or not, she laughed. Being a classmate for a couple of years in medical school she thought she knew me. After laughing, she asked me with a serious face, of all the ladies out there, why her?

I knew from the little I had gathered about her that she wasn't referring to the superficial stuff. She was asking where I was headed and how exactly she fits in that picture. You can imagine going to a lady of such calibre without knowing where you are heading, what you are trying to achieve in this life and how exactly she would fit in. It's a disaster! Luckily, I was prepared for it and it got me the woman.

You Know When Your Doors Open

One other amazing thing about knowing your purpose is that you know your doors open or opportunities come your way. You are not excited just with anything else other than something that connects to your purpose. You are sharp and strategic in looking for your specific opportunities according to your purpose.

There is a story about two brothers in Genesis 27, where the firstborn, Esau was in line to get "the blessing" that was being passed on from one generation to the next. The younger brother, Jacob knew about the blessing and knew that it was a right for the firstborn to receive it. He knew all that he needed was to find an opportunity to be the firstborn to receive it. So, he looked for an opportunity to present itself to get the birthright from his elder brother.

Since he knew what he needed to achieve, he knew exactly the tools required to get it done which included "the blessing" that Isaac – his father, carried. He needed to do whatever it took to get that blessing from Isaac. The purpose defined to him the resources he needed, and he was just waiting for the day he would get the birthright from his elder brother.

Guess what? A day came when his elder brother got hungry and looked for food of which the younger brother had. He offered to give his older brother the food in exchange for the birthright. He didn't have to think twice because this is the opportunity he had been looking for. In the end, the elder brother was foolish enough to trade his birth-right which he regretted for the rest of his life. What tools or resources do you need for the journey?

Not every school or job opportunity, beautiful lady or handsome young man who comes your way is right for you. How do you tell between the right or wrong opportunities among the good that come your way if you don't know what you need to accomplish in the end? Which doors do you hope and pray for and why, if you don't have a destination you are basing that request?

Know Exactly What Is Expected of You
When you know the purpose of something you know exactly what to expect from it. You have your expectations according to what you know it should or shouldn't do. You have the right to be frustrated when something or someone is not functioning per their roles and responsibilities.

When you employ someone, who promises to meet certain job criteria and deliverables, but they don't, you are justified to be frustrated either to train or fire them. God fired king Saul and employed David in his place just because he couldn't deliver on the post.

Imagine a gadget designer who puts and expects certain functions in his or her gadget and it's unable to deliver, it should be heart-breaking. It's the same way how the one who designed you to function in a certain way feels seeing you operate otherwise; doing things you were never meant to do at the expense of the things you should be doing.

When you know your purpose, you know exactly what you owe the world whether the world knows it or not. Even when you do things which the world expected otherwise from you, as long as it is what you are supposed to do for the world then you are good to go. You are not bothered or destructed by what the world says you should be doing. Your body, character, personality, etc, the combination of all that, was specifically made to achieve something.

Reveals Your Identity and Potential
As said earlier, one of the ways you can know the kind of tool you are or should be is by knowing the kind of job that is expected of you. If you know you should be treating the sick chances are high that you are fit to be a doctor. If you know your job is to protect people, then you should be a law enforcer of some kind.

It helps you to define the characteristics, the values and standards you need to set for yourself for you to carry yourself as a tool to accomplish the task that you are meant to. If you are raw material, you start differentiating towards being a tool or a person fit to accomplish that specific thing. The reason no country can take a vendor to run a nation is that he or she isn't developed yet as a tool to run the nation. But he or she can develop into a president material through knowledge, skills and exposure to be fit for the job.

For this very reason, institutions send their employees for additional training whilst they are already working for them. They want them to be a tool to meet a certain demand in the workplace to deliver certain results.

It also reveals to you the potential that you carry within even though you are still raw. David was anointed to be king over Israel at around 16 years of age, but he was still raw at that age. He wasn't fit to lead Israel that's why he needed developing before he could eventually be appointed to be a king. He needed time and process for the king in him to come out. He knew what his purpose was, and he had to work toward being a worthy fit for the role of leading the people of God.

Do you know your potential? Do you know how much you carry in you? All that you can be? If only you get to know your purpose, then you know how much potential you have.

You Know How Best to Use Yourself as a Tool

A great man of God, Dr Myles Munroe in his book "The Pursuit of Purpose" said where there is no purpose tools or resources are bound to be misused. Wise King Solomon said, where there is no vision people (or things) perish. I guess partly because people don't know the actual use for the resources they have at their disposal.

You are a tool with abilities befitting your purpose. Just as at work if you are a secretary who doesn't know how to drive a car, your boss should know that you are not a tool for driving because that's not your job description and you don't have the abilities to do the job. You should be able to tell people when they are misallocating you. Let them know it's not what you are cut out for, instead of accepting to do something you will fail in.

We have heard or seen football players being played out of position and not producing results not because they are not good but because they are asked to deliver something they are not meant for. You find a striker asked to defend and a goalkeeper to play as a striker. Same with you, if you are given a role that you are not fit for you are bound to fail miserably. Don't go for jobs you know you are not fit to deliver; you end up just being a frustrated being and labelled a failure.

When you know your purpose, you know how to position yourself. You don't fight with others for a place just because their role is more exposed and get more recognition. You know exactly what you are cut out for, and where and how you need to serve in the situation. When there is a need for you to be in the background, you are in the background and when it's time for you to be on the podium, you are there according to the purpose you must serve.

When you are a leader in a team, it will save you a great headache when you understand your team first. You should be able to know who is good at what and where everyone does their best work for the greater good. Henry Ford didn't get rich and famous because he was formally educated or knew how to do the actual job but rather because he understood the needs of the job to get done and found the people with certain skills (purposes) and put them in the right place to get it done. His purpose was to assemble a team, a system to bring out the final product.

You get to assemble a team or a system the way it should effectively be because you know how everyone, or everything functions in relation to the other in trying to achieve the greater organization goal.

Offers Independence and Or Originality
Once you know your purpose you get to be in a world of your own. Someone said that everyone is born original but most end up dying copycats. We aren't who we should be because we don't know what we should be living for as individuals.

Have you ever been with someone who knows exactly what they are looking for or what they want?

These people are unshakable; they don't just follow anyone or anything anyhow. They are not easily persuaded to do foolish things or things that don't add value to their lives.

When you know your purpose, you don't go with the multitude, you become whole or independent. You don't even need anyone to define you because you know who you are from within and what you are supposed to accomplish.

You have no time to compete with anyone, except for common limited resources, because you know you have your specific set-path to walk in and specific things to accomplish and enjoy. You may share a home, profession and even be twins but your purposes completely differ.

Why would a CEO compete with a guard in an organization when their job descriptions are completely different? This is exactly how life should be only that most people haven't come to realize their purposes. We have copycats or ignorant people walking through life with no idea of what they should be doing with or in it. Busy competing with others on things they shouldn't even be pursuing.

You don't do a course just because everyone is doing it and you are afraid you would be the only one behind. If it is of no value to your purpose, you know it's just a waste of your time. You don't go for a girl or accept a guy just because every other person likes them. Do they add any value to your purpose?

The purpose that your marriage has determines how you spend your time and resources. You don't have to compare yourself to any other marriage. Whatever they choose to invest in whether food, dressing, leisure, business, etc is none of your business. Focus on your future and what you need to achieve eventually and that should determine how you live your life as a couple.

Knowing your purpose and sticking to it puts you in the driver's seat for your own life and you call the shots when you want to not because someone wants you to. You are the CEO over your life, and you walk in your unique path. Your purpose gives you that originality.

Gives Energy to Keep On

Where your treasure is, your heart is also (Matthews 6:21; Luke 12:34). I didn't understand it in the light of what I want to share with you till now. When you look at something like a treasure you value it and your heart is there, and when your heart is eventually there, its feelings follow. When you have positive feelings about something then nothing else matters around you; you are all about that treasure in every way. You work for it and you never get tired of it, you just want to do more and more. Where feelings are, the energy is in constant supply.

Let me bring in a loose connection to support the issue of value and feelings. Have you ever been close to someone whom you initially never thought of dating but after spending time with them you start developing feelings for them? You know why? Because you have seen the value in them, you have seen the treasure in them beyond the body and your heart goes there and feelings start to develop for them. It's the same thing with an endeavour when it has a value in terms of purpose in it. You develop a passion for it.

In one of my favourite movies, "The 3 Idiots", Papa Racho said - I will paraphrase it – "if you make your passion your job, then work becomes play." Meaning once you understand your purpose and find a job that's line with it you look forward to every morning to go to work. Your energy levels never run dry because even though you labour more than most at the workplace you never tire; the feelings supply the needed energy and mood to get the job done.

Purpose is the life that successful and completed journeys are made of. It is what energizes conviction which in turn is a force that can never be bought or tamed. When the going gets tough, it is the desire to see purpose through that keeps people going. It is the purpose that easily gives people hope and determination to push on until they see what they are fighting for come to pass. It is mostly purpose that let soldiers put their lives on the line for others. It is the purpose that made Nelson Mandela, Gandhi, John Chilembwe, Malcolm X, Steve Biko endure hardship till they saw people's freedom or tilted the scales to plant seeds that would ensure that freedom.

You can think of any area of life, once it's purpose-driven, you make it work without complaining. You don't look for reasons why you can't make it work but rather ways to make it work. I am of the idea that some relationships are not working because other than having fun and having the "in relationship" status, there is nothing much to it. Taking away your loneliness is not a reason enough to start, let alone sustain a relationship. When he or she is there, and you no longer feel lonely he or she no longer has any use in your life.

The purpose you had (ending loneliness) was for someone not in a relationship, not one in it, hence you don't find a reason to continue in it. Then we wonder why breakups are on the rise, I think the answer could be purpose or lack thereof. When there is a well-defined purpose, you invest and work towards it as a team. Relationships wouldn't die easily, not from internal or external forces. You become a team that fights against whatever forces try to come between you. If you are in a relationship or marriage, have a common purpose or direction and agree to push towards it as a team and see the effect of having something bigger than the relationship, marriage and family.

Studies have shown that people without purpose are more likely to die earlier than those with a sense of purpose in life. I believe people commit suicide because they have nothing to live or die for. Circumstances don't warrant suicide lack of purpose in life does. One who has purpose does everything despite the circumstances to see their purpose through. They know that their lives have meaning regardless of the present circumstances.

I worked hard in school as a child not because I had everything but because I knew I had something to accomplish through school. I could go to primary and secondary school without pocket money and sometimes without school fees in secondary, but never did I think of quitting, why? Because as a child after a little exposure from Illovo employees (then SUCOMA), I "set" a purpose to push on. The purpose was to be a boss someday, make a lot of money from work and rescue my family and I from the pangs of lack.

That purpose gave me the energy to keep on and keep fighting all the way regardless of the resources I lacked.

Mostly, those that struggle with school haven't yet found a purpose for school. It doesn't matter whether they are from rich or poor families but if they don't see school adding any value to something in their lives, they don't have a reason to push for it; it's not just an issue of IQ and learning techniques. If you show these children how school adds value to their lives, then you will see how things can turn around. Everyone is intelligent and because of that everyone can find their best way of learning and push through school. Different study techniques work almost for everyone; everyone has a chance to make it in school if they are willing to.

I lost my interest in medical school when I was in my second year and I had no reason to push on because I thought medical education wasn't adding anything to my purpose. If it wasn't for my mentor who helped me find the significance of my first degree, then I would have given up. It felt like a waste of my precious time. I had to find out what my first degree would serve towards my purpose.

Finally, I got it. It wasn't about clinical knowledge and skills but interaction with patients and the doors my first degree would open for me that kept me going. It wasn't easy and because of that I drugged through college and it was easy for my lecturers to notice one way or the other that I wasn't very much interested. When it came to clinical work, I was an average student and usually produced half-baked work, yet there was something more valuable to me that I learnt aside from the clinical knowledge and skills. The process through medical school built something in me that's helping me excel in my non-clinical work.

I remember when I was in Paediatrics rotation, I was late for class and I bumped into my lecturer and rotation mentor, Dr Margot Anderson. She said, "Khuwi, it's not too late to quit and do something you love, I know most students are forced by their parent to do medicine". She could tell that I lacked the fire and excitement in my education. But still, I had to find a reason to push to the end to get my first degree.

If you read finance books by finance gurus such as Robert Kiyosaki, they always say that purpose or mission for the business is one of the main reasons they survive beyond 3 years from their inception. If you go to such people with a business idea, they will first ask you the purpose that the business will serve. These guys know the power of a purpose.

I read a story about Edwin Barnes who had nothing, not even money for a train fare to meet the business guru – Andrew Carnegie who he wanted to partner with. In addition to that when he finally got to his destination, he had to work for at least 5 years in menial jobs which didn't matter to Carnegie. All the effort he put in for 5 years still didn't get him any closer to his desire. Regardless of such lack of progress, he persisted for years, with his eyes on the end picture, waiting for his door to open. Finally, he got what he was pushing for when a door opened.

Brings and Keeps People or Things Together

Purpose has the power to bring people from different walks of life to stand together for a common goal. It binds even people that have never met before. A good example is of the demonstrators in reaction to the Malawi Presidential Election that took place in Malawi on the 21st May 2019. Most of them were people that never knew each other till this day but still stood together for a cause bigger than each one of them. Every one of them individually couldn't stand the injustice that had happened to humankind and because of the common purpose to see justice prevail they came together and fought for justice to the end.

Everyone who wasn't happy played their role towards a common goal of overturning the results for re-election. Starting from the petitioners, prayer warriors, lawyers, judges, HRDC, soldiers, leaders of oppositions, witnesses and even mere men.

Purpose is one of the main things that have kept my relationship going even in the toughest of times. We are bound by something bigger than our minor differences. My wife is my treasure because she is my purpose buddy, and where my treasure is, my heart is also, hence very easy to constantly love her. A relationship is not just about the anatomy, physiology and the chemistry but more so about the purpose that binds you two. When I was writing this book, she (my wife) asked me how we managed to keep our long-distance relationship going. We could see each other once in one to three months in the 3 years we dated but here we are happily married. I answered her that it's because we had a purpose in our relationship, something to look forward to. This is how powerful purpose is.

In the 3 years we courted, we never kissed nor slept together before marriage yet still loved each other. This is all because we knew eventually that sex would come in after marriage, but we still had a force that bonded us together whether sex was there or not. What our union has set out to achieve is far more important than the children we may or may not have and the money we may and may not have. Everything else is added to the purpose behind our agreement to walk together towards.

Some marriages that are not working could be because of the absence of purpose or sense of common direction. God created man to be the head of the marriage and eventually a family. It's not about how much a woman earns or how reputable she is but when it comes to a household then there should be a head of the family and that's the man. A woman can fund a common purpose for the family from money she makes from work but still respects the husband as the head of the family business in terms of direction. Not that a man is more important than a woman, everyone is significant in their way and roles.

The reason behind marriage is that you should become one entity, with one direction but with more abilities in dealing with a common purpose. Imagine your goal is to cover an area of ground. Whether one person or two do it the reward would be the same for each one of you individually whether you do it as a team or not. So, you end up being paid the full amount for half the effort you put in because you have combined your efforts.

I think when there is a sense of direction (plans), women find it easy to submit to their husbands. You need to work as a team and put your resources including the acquired knowledge, skills, time, mind and money towards this purpose (direction). When you have a sense of purpose as a team with well -defined roles and responsibilities, I believe it's hard to think about divorce. With a common purpose, I don't think there could be ulterior motives amongst you. You have something to focus on and push for and are both doing your part, according to your skills and talents. One is attacking and the other is defending to win a game of life as a team.

One of the reasons people walk out of political parties or business partnerships is because either there was no purpose, to begin with, or it was lost along the way. There is no basis for these people to continue together anymore.

When you know your purpose, you know which people to associate with or spend time with and stick to, which coaches or mentors to follow, which church to be in, which seminars to be attending and which information to get glued to.

Helps You Realize How Best You Fit in A System
When companies or organization systems are made, roles are created with their corresponding responsibilities. This helps people know exactly how they fit in the systems within an institution.

I believe one other reason why marriages and families fall apart is that either the roles and responsibilities are not clearly defined, or someone is not playing his or her role per their expected responsibilities. Every role in a marriage and or family has their corresponding responsibilities of which if everyone stuck to them, I believe, there wouldn't have been contention amongst family members which sometimes lead to divorce. What's your role as a husband and father, as a wife and mother, as a son and brother, and as a daughter and sister?

For the same reason, before people get into a relationship just as they do with a job application, they have first to understand what their roles and responsibilities are or will be and that of the other side. As a man, you should understand who a man is and what his responsibilities are but also understand a woman and what her responsibilities are or should be, and vice versa. That way you know how best your responsibilities complement each other for a greater good. You can also agree on what each other's responsibilities should be.

Know how you fit at work, at home, in your community, church, school and generally in life according to the needs, gap or opportunities in the places you are, and in line with the natural desires and skills that you have and can apply.

When you know your purpose, you know exactly where you fit in at home, church, community, workplace, and you don't have to fight or compete with anyone. You know when exactly you are needed to do something about a situation, and you know the thing you should do.

During the fight for the presidential election case, some fought their battles through prayer in their war rooms, others in the courtroom, others on their computers digging up evidence, whilst others were in the street demonstrating or protecting demonstrators. Everyone fought for a common purpose per their knowledge and abilities. If anyone of them was misplaced, chances are high that it could have been a disaster.

Determines How You Build or Prepare Yourself

If you have never been at a construction site, try to do so and compare the kinds of foundations needed for a skyscraper and a one-story building. The depth and design of the foundation are determined by the purpose both the foundation and the building to be constructed will serve.

If you know you are to carry the responsibility of a skyscraper in you then dig deep into your foundation through having a strong identity, developing strong character, personality, deeper and wider knowledge and skill base. You can't prepare for life just like any other Jim and Jack out there. You are different and special therefore you need special preparation.

As a football player, you can't be practising the way a chess player does just because both of you are players. There will be a few common things to do with mental preparation, but the rest of the physical exercise and strategies will be different between the two of you. So, why compare yourself to them through their preparation process, and why join them and expect to excel as if you are facing the same challenges?

You can't go through the process that produces a doctor and expect to come out as an engineer, pastor or businessman. These people are going to serve completely different purposes therefore why go through the same refining process? Look at how princes and princesses are raised in England and see if it's the same process with the rest of their English Citizens. It's completely different because they have different purposes to serve.

When you understand the uniqueness of purpose you don't prepare like everyone else. Don't try to fit in. You have too much to lose. With this, you also realize that everyone has their purpose, and you help them per their needs. You know who needs to go through what and why. You don't treat your children or friends the same because you know everyone has his or her purpose to serve which means they need individualized support.

Determines the Fulfilment and Peace of Soul
Even though people achieve somewhat great things in life such as great businesses, career or "ministry" yet still feel to have missed the mark is because they left the purpose aside.

Even though we think that money answers all things but how we spend that money sooner or later catches up with us. The reason old billionaires give out their money for noble causes, even though they have children and grandchildren to inherit it, is that they have come to realize that there was a course they needed to pursue which they didn't. They don't have peace to check out of the earth without meeting that need in their souls. It's not about fame or respect but the difference they want to make to humankind after realizing what matters in life.

Since life is a journey it's possible to check out before you reach your destination. Death isn't your destination. If you die before you reach your destination it means your destiny has been aborted. What will you have to show for before you check out the earth that has impacted and made a difference for the inhabitants on the earth?

Dr Myles Munroe said that life is not measured in the length of years lived but how much of purpose has been fulfilled or remains to be fulfilled. Your life should be purpose-driven than years lived. You can live a short life yet rich, impactful and fulfilling as Jesus did. The King of Wakanda lived 44 years but we have seen and felt the impact he has made. This is all that matters not length of life. We exist to leave a mark on earth even though it isn't our eternal home.

❦ DISCOVERING YOU PURPOSE

Chapter Eight

'"Ask, and it will be given to you; seek, and you will find; knock, and it will be opened to you. For everyone who asks receives, and the one who seeks finds, and to the one who knocks it will be opened.' **Matthew 7:7-8 ESV**

"How then do I know my purpose?" This is the question that has puzzled many people throughout their lives and civilizations. For Christians and those who believe that there is God, asking your God is the best place to start from. For the sake of everyone else, I will share with you how you can get a glimpse of or know your purpose.

Before I start this topic let me point out that you can get to know your purpose by using any of these elements but if it falls under several of them the more you are on track. Combination of these things narrows down your real purpose.

Just like the interconnected systems that aid each other, make sure that what you are doing is something that is making a difference and adding value to the world around you, just as other people's impact affects your life. The idea is to form an interlinked system that supports each other for the greater good of the earth.

Fulfilment or Satisfaction When Done

One thing that is common to purpose is that when you do something related to it you have a sense of fulfilment or accomplishment or joy that nothing else can bring. It is one positive thing or things that you would do without being paid for, or one thing you would still do if you have all or no money in your life.

We all have something good and right that makes us feel all sorts of nice when we accomplish it. No matter how demanding or tiresome it can be, but we still smile at the end of the day because of the difference we have made. Some get it when they are treating patients in the hospital, others when they give to the poor, others when they see justice prevail whilst others when they lead and make things happen.

You should find out from the things you do that make you feel like you are walking on the moon; the ones that give you a feeling of euphoria. Something that makes you forget that people get tired and feel hungry when you are absorbed into it, for the sake of the world around you.

For Jesus (Luke 4:43) and Paul, it was preaching the gospel and planting churches. For Dorcas, it was charity work (Acts 9:36), for Mandela and Gandhi was the freedom of their fellow countrymen and for the likes of Bill and Melinda Gates funding the fight against deadly diseases.

Things That Evoke Anger in You

Sometimes it is through realizing what makes you angry or concerns you when you see it happening or not happening. For example, in the Bible, there is a story of Nehemiah who was angry when he heard that the walls of Jerusalem were destroyed. He had to leave his comfort to rebuild the walls of Jerusalem. You would be like, so just building a wall can be a purpose, no! The purpose was in what the wall served which is the protection of the people in the city. He couldn't stand the thought of having the city unprotected from their enemies. He just had to do something about it.

Most of us know the story of Nelson Mandela, one of the few great African leaders to have ever lived. He had a purpose to see black -men free from white man's oppression. He was given offers that would have made him a comfortable man, but he turned them down because what gave him peace and fulfilment was something more important and valuable than the physical comfort that the whites promised to give him. Unfortunately, we have a lot of people who settle once they have been offered good things.

Morgan Tsvangirai who was prime minister of Zimbabwe from 2009 and 2013 somewhat settled. He took a journey as a president of the Movement for Democratic Change to rescue Zimbabweans from the oppressive power of late Mr Robert Mugabe. After the 2009 elections, which he supposedly won, Mugabe offered him a prime minister position which he couldn't resist. If his desire was truly to see to it that the democratic change happened in Zimbabwe, he wouldn't have settled but ought to the end even if it meant death.

This is very common with freedom fighters. They rise because they can't stand oppression. Aside from Mandela, we have Malawian President Dr Lazarus Chakwera, Gandhi, Chilembwe, Dr David Livingston among others. These are people who rose and said enough is enough.

Look at David when he came to the Israelites camp, he didn't have to think twice seeing Goliath defying the armies of the Living God (1 Samuel 17:26). He couldn't help it but be angry for his God and the oppression of his people. It wasn't about the reward after killing Goliath but the anger that was welling up in him. He would rather die than watching Goliath continue insulting His God. That is what purpose should do to you; it should be a fire in you and something you live for and willing to die for if need be.

What is it that you don't like when you see happening around you? Is it oppression like for the people above? Is it sickness or injustice? What are you equipped with to fight against such things you hate to make the world a better place? If it makes you mad it might as well be because there is a solution placed in you. You don't have to sit on it because people's lives depend on you.

What Are You Naturally Good At?

Understanding or figuring out your natural talents is one of the ways you can figure out what your purpose is. Search within yourself things you are goods at naturally. How do the skills or talents fit into your environment by adding value or make things better for others? You may be paid for them or not, but the main thing is adding value and making a difference.

Blessed are those whose purpose is within their money-making abilities for they focus on one thing. They are paid for fulfilling their purpose.

You may have a common purpose with other people but how you fit therein depends on the skills you have. I gave an example of how purpose united people during the Malawi presidential election case, and how everyone fits in their roles according to their skills.

Let me agree with the statement that Dr Myles Munroe said, the skills or the abilities you have determine the purpose you need to serve. In addition to his statement, I will say "the skills or talents and the abilities you have are not your purpose but rather reveal how you may realize your purpose or fit in a bigger purpose." They reveal more about your vision, the means or tool through which your purpose will be fulfilled or channelled. Don't worry I will expand more about vision in the next chapter.

This is my first time to write a book and will be followed by several others already written. Despite achieving this feat, I am not surprised that I have done this. I am a person who has loved writing since my secondary school days. Not English literature kind of writings but rather the things that I have learnt or interest me.

Writing a book is tedious work but I enjoy it because aside from having a purpose in me to teach, I have skills that enable me to fulfil my teaching through writing a book. Writing is a means to disseminate information, knowledge or wisdom, and if I have the skill to write it means there is something in me that has to come out through my writing.

Let me emphasize this, your natural-born talent or skills are not your purpose, they are a means to meeting your purpose. How you direct your talents and skills determines whether you meet your purpose or not. Singing is not a purpose but the message you sing and the impact and the difference you make on people's lives with your message, that's your purpose.

You can be a singer who hates gender-based violence or would want people to live healthy lives. So, you compose songs that address such things. Purpose is meant to address something that people are going or may go through to avoid it and make life better for them.

Past Experiences

"Sometimes you need to feel the sting of pain and sting of defeat to activate the real passion and purpose that God predestined inside of you... Whatever you choose for a career path, remember, the struggles along the way are only meant to shape you for your purpose." **Chad-**

wick Boseman – Howard University Commencement Speech

Purpose can be realized through the pain and the wounds that we have gone through. Through those scars, we are better placed to help others either to avoid the same fate or to help those that are in the process. You become a beacon of hope to those who are amidst the storm; a living testimony that hard times don't last.

It's not just about negative things, even the good path you have taken to success, you help others to be successful too. With your help, you make their lives better and prevent a lot of other things that could go wrong from their despair and their pain. Use those scars the right way; scars of heartbreak, rejection, poverty, physical scars and whatever scars you may have. Don't hide them, use them to make a difference! On the other hand, the spiritual, material and educational success you have attained isn't just for you, you need to help others to attain similar success as well.

I recently watched a movie, Just Mercy, by Michael B. Jordan which was based on a true story of Bryan Stevenson who is an American lawyer. Bryan grew up in the early 1960s when segregation against black people in America, due to racism, was at the peak. He said he grew up wondering and asking himself the question of why people are judged or treated unfairly because of their skin colour. Because of the experience he went through, he understood how segregation feels like.

After he graduated from law school, he found the Equal Justice Initiative in Montgomery, Alabama which aside from working to change sentences for death row inmates he also has made efforts to challenge racial discrimination in the justice system which is part of the racial unfairness he grew up facing. Through the painful experience, he went through and discovered his purpose therein.

Blair Hill, Napoleon Hill's son, was born partially deaf. He didn't have ear canals on his skull – the skull bone didn't have openings to connect the outside of the ear to the inner part of the ear. This didn't stop his parents from searching for ways to help him hear properly. After their hard-earned efforts paid off, Blair Hill used his hardship to make a difference to other deaf people by helping them to hear. To him, it wasn't just about making money. He chose to market, for the company that developed the hearing aid, the device that made a difference to him. Through a hard time, he went through and he chose to make a difference to others who were in a similar situation of despair from lack or loss of hearing.

We need to learn to draw lessons from the circumstances we are going through instead of just complaining about them or celebrating them when they happen to us. There is always a reason you had to go through that process. It's not just for you but to somehow help others for a better life experience. Best mentors, in any area of life, are those who have walked the journey and talk the walk; good or bad. Draw lessons from your experiences.

Through Those Around You

You can discover your purpose through people suggesting to you or telling you what stands out in you. There is a tendency in man to overlook the good in them and admire the good in others. You can take advantage of this character trait in man to your advantage by asking people what they admire most or see in you, and you work around that.

Ask people around you for their opinion to show you what you are good at or driven by. They may be better positioned to point things out just as we can do to others.

Mentors, coaches and parents better understand things and are sometimes able to see things that you can't; they can put two and two together for you. There is an African Proverb that says, "What elders see whilst sitting, a young person can't see whilst standing." Not that the elders are taller even from a sitting position rather because they have the experience and a third eye to see beyond and understand what you can't.

Caution, it doesn't mean everything that people tell you, you should jump into it. As I said they may help point something out, but you still make your soul searching if what they are saying is true and if you need to go into that direction.

Circumstances Around You

By looking at problems around you and how you can be a solution to them gives you an idea what your purpose is. Usually, we have purposes at different stages which we should meet as we go to meet even a greater purpose in the years ahead.

It's not just about how you can be a solution per se but rather how or if you fit in being part of the solution. It's about playing your role in the whole picture. You may be the main character in one scenario, supporting in another and behind the scenes in another depending on your skills, availability and resources that you should solve the problem at hand. It gets a little similar to seeing something you don't like happening around you because both are about meeting a need. Only that this time you may not necessarily be angry about the problem, but you can notice the gap and you are happy to bridge it with the solutions that you have. This usually happens in the business world, but it can also happen at the workplace, church, family, in your community, district, nation, continent and even the whole world.

Through the Word of God

I wouldn't want to leave any stone unturned. To my fellow Christians, aside from the above ways to discover your purpose, you also have the Bible or the word of God that enlightens you on your direction.

There are other ways in Christianity such as prophecy – in case of Jesus, dreams – for Joseph, from a man of God – the case of David, the word from God to parents - the case of Samson, encounter – the case of Paul,

Zachariah (John's father - through prayer and worship, etc. There are so many ways how people from the beginning of the world discovered their purposes or callings, and you can search that in the Bible.

Purpose, calling and assignment are all the same thing and have the same reward when accomplished. It is paramount that as a Christian you get your assignment that aligns with the plans of your King and His Kingdom. I have written a book specifically on this topic for Christians titled, "Christian's Purpose" which centres on the Kingdom of God and our roles and responsibilities as citizens in His Kingdom. Please grab your copy if you want to know where you stand in the Kingdom.

🌿 BE PURPOSE CONSCIOUS

Chapter Nine

Now that you know that life is purpose-driven, I want you to be purpose conscious in every place that you are. It is your responsibility as a person to make sure that you are equipped to handle your roles at work, home, church, etc but even more so to the world.

It's not just about you benefiting from the family, organization, church but also you playing your role and serving your purpose. In the end, pushing the whole institution forward along with its purpose or mission through the meeting of their purpose-driven goals.

Before you proceed to the next chapter please sit down and sort out this area first if not yet sorted. You will not discover your purpose in one sitting, let alone know where best it fits in the society or world, but you should at least start searching. Ask yourself the following:

- What is my purpose?
- What am I naturally good at?
- What do I enjoy doing?
- What have you gone through that you can help people with?
- What gives me a sense of fulfilment when I do or see others doing it?

- What is it that you can't stand and what can you do about it according to the skills and talents you have?
- What do people say you are good at?

When you study the word of God or when listening to teachings, what fills your spirit within with excitement or anger and see yourself doing something about it?

The more you find something that answers all the above questions the better. I am a medical doctor who loves and enjoys helping people but not in the hospital setting. I have my ways of helping people but not patients or just not as a medical doctor, and because of that, I had to move out of the hospital and go into something that I know best and enjoy doing. Despite patients, guardians and colleagues telling me that I am a good doctor and needed to be in the hospital, I had to assess myself and go the way I know I would enjoy for the rest of my life and be where I know I best fit.

Remember it boils down to the tools you have at your disposal? Fight per the skills and abilities at your disposal. If you are a writer then write against it, if you are an artist sing against it, if you are a lawyer apply for a petition against it, if you are a philanthropist fund those that are fighting directly against it.

Bill and Melinda Gates have been fighting against a lot of diseases all over the world, but they don't have to be in the hospital for it. They fight according to their ability which is funding those on the ground. Even for those on the ground, not everyone works in the hospital treating the sick; others are in the communities or behind computers fighting to prevent people from getting infected in the first place, finding better treatments, etc. Same purpose but different skills targeting different areas.

It won't help you, in the long run, to be in a place where you earn praise or money whilst you are dying within your soul. Every day you get drained because of the things you are facing, and the natural talents and desires you don't have for the job. Life is made easier, enjoyable and fulfilling in purpose, discover it!

MISSION STATEMENT

Chapter Ten

"A mission statement should clearly define and crystalize the organization's (or personal) purpose, philosophy, and goals." **Dr Myles Munroe – Rediscovering the Kingdom**

Mission statements, vision and goals confuse a lot of people. Often, they are presented in a way that is hard for most people to grasp the concept. A mission statement is an abstract for your life – a summary that covers the key activities or achievements to be done along life's journey. It reflects on the how's and why's. Everyone is on a mission to achieve something. What keeps you awake at night? What passion seeps through your veins and causes a fire in your bones? Beyond the 'what', 'how' do you plan to achieve it?

Just like any organization, you need to make your mission statement clear to everyone who wants to work or partner with you, your friends, your life partner, relatives and workmates. Those around you should know what you are about, who you are, where you are going and what you want to achieve at the end of it all. In doing so people will know how to relate with you and know the things they need to include you in if they are within your scope of purpose or not. We tend to be accessible to a lot of things without truly reflecting how the things we are opening ourselves to mirror with our purpose.

Look at the one person who heartily accomplished His purpose for three and a half years from the time He started working on it:

"The Spirit of the Lord is upon me because he has anointed me to proclaim good news to the poor. He has sent me to proclaim liberty to the captives and recovering of sight to the blind, to set at liberty those who are oppressed, to proclaim the year of the Lord's favour." **Luke 4:18-19**

Jesus never did anything outside of that mission statement. Everything that He did was within that scope. It served as a basis for His decisions and actions. No wonder He made such a huge impact that is still transforming the world today.

What are you equipped to do? How are you going to do it? What is your end? Write down that mission statement. Memorize it. Meditate on it. Let it guide you. Let those around you know it. Every successful organization has a mission statement. You are an organization encompassing different departments and systems. The fundamental question remains: for the journey that you have embarked on, what is your mission statement?

❦ VISION

Chapter Eleven

"But rise and stand on your feet, for I have appeared to you for this purpose, to make you a minister and a witness both of what you saw, and in what I shall appear to you..." **Acts 26:16**

"And we know that for those who love God all things work together for good, for those who are called according to his purpose. For those whom he foreknew, he also predestined" **Romans 8:28-29**

As mentioned at the beginning, living life is like taking a journey to the future. Even though purpose may be the heart of the journey the vision is the destination for the journey, your destiny, where you wish to end up.

The purpose is the intangible goal you achieve through your efforts. In an implementation research sense, purpose (or aim) would be defined as the outcome and its impact (the things that an output can achieve). Inputs would be the things you need to do for you to be an effective 'output.' From input (resources) or to an output (vision) to an outcome (what the output can do - the purpose). This all boils down to impact (the effect of the purpose).

A vision is more of an end picture whilst a purpose

is what that end picture serves, does, accomplishes or the difference it makes. Since vision is an end picture that's why it's called vision because it's something that you can see with your eyes. If you see yourself as a lawyer in 10 years' time, that's not a purpose but rather a vision. What you will do when you become a lawyer, that's your purpose.

From the first piece of scriptures above you will see that the purpose of the Lord's visit was to make Paul a vision (minister) and give him a purpose. A vision is a tool with characteristics, potential and abilities to meet a certain purpose. Jesus had a vision of Paul being a witness and a minister of the gospel. Being a witness or a minister is a vision but witnessing, ministering and converting people to Jesus that was Paul's purpose.

If you want to have a healthy community, you would either choose to be a doctor to treat patients or you would choose to open a clinic or a hospital and employ healthcare workers to treat patients. Despite whatever visible way (vision) you choose to go by, in the end, your community will be treated and have healthy people – purpose and impact. Being a doctor or building a clinic is the vision. What they do however is the purpose.

This is what the second piece of scripture is conveying. Being foreknown of God entails who you are and who

you should be. This is fundamental to accomplishing

your purpose. God knows you cannot do something well until you first become all that He has called you to be. Before leading, you cannot lead until you are a leader first. Paul couldn't preach or minister well until he was made a minister first.

The tragedy of Not Having Your Vision

In this life, it is those with a vision that call the shots. Vision helps a person to be deliberate and know why they are doing certain things. Those that vision relentlessly pursues their hearts desire with much passion. If you are not chasing your vision surely someone is using you to meet theirs.

Truth is, it's either you are pursuing your vision and destiny or someone else's. It is all up to you. Your choices. Your decisions. It is purpose and vision that mainly give intent, motivation and focus on doing certain things. Without that, you get to be all over the place. You are busy yet not productive. At the end of the day, week or year you are tired of doing nothing because you have no idea what you are working for or building towards. You look back after a year and you realize you have nothing to show for the 365 days that have passed.

A man with a vision is a step further than a man with only a purpose. Vision is what makes a purpose a reality. It gives you something you can work with. Vision is about the outlook of your life. It is about the things you would want to be or possess to meet your purpose. Goal setting aids in placing appropriate timelines to the vision.

Vision Capturing in Every Area of Life

You need to capture and set a vision in every area of your life. You can't leave any area of your life to chance because we become what we envision with our minds. Envision the structure of your life, how it will be and how each area will look like and relate to your purpose. What things would you want to possess?

Vision acts as a script for your life which you and you alone should write. People will write wrong scripts for you on how to live your life if you let them to because they don't understand your purpose and your desires. You alone should write your own script of what you would want to walk in, achieve and how your life should be according to your purpose.

Define the people you would want to have around you and the type of job you would want to be in and the type of car to drive. Henry Kachaje also recommends the same in his program - "Succeed Young", for the youths. After defining this, you should start living this life. From here you know the resources, people and the type of knowledge and skills you need. You should know the next step from where you are to take you to the next chapter of life.

❦ GOALS AND GOAL SETTING

Chapter Twelve

"Success is the progressive realization of a worthy goal or ideal." **Earl Nightingale**

A goal is an end product, something you want to achieve at the end of all your activities. The why to your actions. It could be starting a business, getting into a relationship, building a circle of friends, getting a car, and marrying. Ideally, every goal must be as vivid as possible, clearly depicting what you are trying to do. Josh Kaufman in his book "The Personal MBA", said a goal must be framed in PICS format- Positive, Immediate, Concrete and Specific.

Positive: it should motivate you - something that draws you closer to it not one that pushes you away. You shouldn't set freeing goals. You don't go far. Not "I don't want to be single" but "I want to be in a relation-ship".

Immediate: it should be something you decide to work on now rather than later. The things that you wish to embark on should be on your wish-list and should not be considered as goals. A goal is a now-thing, not someday.

Concrete: This means you will have a clear measur-able result; starting a business, going to the USA or

getting a car. These are the things which you know when they happen. You can pinpoint them.
Specific: This is the when, the where and the how of your goals.

You also need to carefully consider the resources needed to achieve your goals: the people you might need to work with; who will be responsible for each task; the knowledge and skills needed; the possible challenges you may face in trying to meet your goal; how to overcome them.

You can set goals in any area of your life. Whether in relationships, spirituality, ministry, family, career and finances. So long as they have the PICS format, you will be assured of better success. You need to make sure that the goals are in line with the ultimate purpose of your life. The ultimate goal is to run your life as one connected system that holistically moves in unison towards your purpose.

Just like any organization, your life needs an ultimate goal (purpose) and a mission. You want to buy a car, why? You want to be married, to whom and why? How do all these things fit into your journey and achieve the ultimate goal? Are they wrought from a real need or an impulsive want?

How To Tackle Your Big Or Ultimate Goals
You can plan such life goals in what is known as "Result Framework" or "Strategic Framework". Result framework is where you have a strategic objective or ultimate goal i.e

the long-term goal. What's your ultimate goal in finances, career, business, relationship or marriage, ministry, etc. From the ultimate goal, you walk backwards looking at the things you need to have, the skills to acquire, money to raise, etc for you to get to that ultimate goal. And you go further backwards and find out the things you need to do or acquire for you to get the resources you need to reach your next goal. So, the resources and qualifications you need to acquire to enable you to pursue the next level goal are your immediate goal or results. So, you have immediate goals which help you reach your intermediate goals which equip you for the long-term goals. [To learn more about types of frameworks for project planning, monitoring and evaluation, you can read the Monitoring and Evaluation Fundamentals booklet by WHO]

Assume you are in secondary or high school and you want to be a professor of law. What's the immediate qualification you need to have before you become a professor? PhD in law. What is the qualification you need before PhD? Master's Degree in law. How about before Master's in Law? Law Degree. Finally, you need a high school or secondary school certificate for you to go to study for a Law Degree.

So, from secondary school, your immediate result is getting a secondary school certificate which will qualify you to go for the Law Degree. In this case, the law degree becomes your immediate goal after you are done with secondary school and so on. Whatever result you desire in any area of life, ask yourself the knowledge, skills or resources you require to make it a reality and ask yourself what you need to do to get those resources, keep on asking yourself a step lower till you get to the things you can do now to get to the next level.

The other advantage of this approach is that each immediate goal or result you achieve serves as an indicator for your progress, it's a milestone achieved. It also serves as landmarks on whether you are on the right track (or not). It also aids in informing you of how close you are to reaching your main goal. Immediate and intermediate goals act as stepping stones to what you want to eventually achieve.

It is impossible to eat an elephant in one go. The only way you can go about it is by eating small chunks at a time. You can't meet your ultimate purpose in one go. You will need to accomplish it step by step through learning, training, overcoming challenges and achieving immediate goals.

Just as an organization that has different departments with unique goals that eventually add to an organization's purpose or mission, all the goals in different areas of your life should support your purpose.

You put your vision and purpose in jeopardy when any area of your life is not properly functioning or managed. If your human resource department goals are not right, you bring wrong partners, friends and mentors into your life's project. Your life can be messed up because of the wrong goals set.

If your finance department targets aren't right, you can't support your purpose. If the monitoring and evaluation department goals aren't optimum, you will keep friends that need to go or accept wrong things. Besides, as a person, you need personal development goals in your quality improvement department (knowledge acquisition, skill development, decision making and goal execution).

"The thing about goals is that living without them is a lot more fun, in the short run. It seems to me, though, that the people who get things done, who lead, who grow and who make an impact.... Those people have goals (set)." **Seth Godin**

Start Small

I know most people are not in the culture of goal setting and prefer their lives to be on autopilot. Though 'living in the moment' is trending, one needs to consider 'tomorrow.' Start by setting small achievable goals. Simplicity forms the skeleton of any plan. Remain consistent and it will all soon flesh out. Plan for small things like buying an inexpensive shoe. You plan when you would want to buy it, why you want to buy it, how you are going to raise funds and where you are buying it. Find out the prices and the challenges along the way and how you plan to tackle them.

THEME TWO:

DEPARTMENTS OF YOUR LIFE

"Imagine your life is perfect in every respect; what would it look like?" – **Brian Tracy**

To live an effective life, one must make sure that all essential areas of life are firing because the areas that aren't will be your downfall. Be healthy, stand spiritually, be good at work, home and be wise at money-making and management. In this section, I will point out some areas of life that I believe are a must to get and keep them functional for true success and happiness.

One area I didn't talk about in this book is health. In all that we do, we need to prioritize our health. Remember that health is not just the absence of physical illness but more so our emotional and mental well-being. Don't seek success to the detriment of your health. You need your health intact to enjoy your success. Eat healthy, exercise and have healthy relationships.

"To keep the body in good health is a duty…otherwise we shall not be able to keep our mind strong and clear" **Buddha Quotes**

SPIRITUAL DEPARTMENT

Chapter Thirteen

"Deep in the human subconscious is a pervasive need for a logical universe that makes sense. But the real universe is always one step beyond logic." **Frank Herbert, Dune**

There are natural and spiritual principles that govern the universe. Just as natural principles or laws directly affect the physical happenings the spiritual principles affect life from a deeper level. Natural laws or principles include the principle of gravity, inertia, action and reaction, sowing and reaping, wear and tear, etc. Spiritual principles include faith, sowing and reaping, love, humility, honesty, among others.

Just as natural principles affect our lives according to whether we obey or disobey them, the spiritual laws have a similar effect only that their physical effects or consequences are usually gradual and manifest fully after some time. Suffice to say that, just like natural principles, spiritual principles don't apply only to those who believe there is God. They are operational to those who believe in and obey them. Principles can never be broken; we just break ourselves against them. To every principle, there is a consequence attached, either a reward or a punishment depending on whether we obey or not.

Dictionary defines spirituality as immateriality; spiritual mindedness; concern with things of the spirit. Spirituality is your ability to be aware of spiritual principles and forces and live in line with them. To be conscious and able to operate from the spiritual realm through observation of spiritual principles and events happening in the spiritual realm.

Spirituality is the foundation, core and essence of a human being because your spirituality or how you observe the spiritual principles determines not only who you are but also the outcome of your life in the physical. Ideally, it determines who you are – character, personality, belief system, values, governing principles. It works at your core and shapes your soul.

People still apply and benefit from the principle of faith even if they don't acknowledge the existence of God. They have no idea of the origin of the principles they are applying or following and benefiting from. All they know is that they make sense to be applied. They apply the principle of faith in invention and business every day and benefit from it. Even the principle of meditation which is commonly and widely used by many is a spiritual principle.

We have read or heard stories from the Bible that God prospered non-believers, even Cornelius from Joppa who wasn't a Born-Again Christian was prosperous from observing the principles of God. Benefiting from the principles of God and salvation are two different things and that's why, despite all the obedience to the principles of God, God still wanted Cornelius to be saved (Acts 10). Let me share with you a big secret, all these successes and personal development principles that motivation speakers use are spiritual principles and are in the Bible. For example, what is referred to as a positive attitude is faith and hope in spirituality. Or it's their product.

If you read Think and Grow Rich by Napoleon Hill, you will realize that it's full of biblical principles of success. The success principles in the Bible are not just for Christians, they are principles on how life should be and how one can operate at his or her optimum level to produce the best results. They are the standard operating procedures for living a fulfilled, successful and sustained life on earth. These are the principles the creator put in place to govern the universe. We need to know them to align ourselves to them to benefit from them the right way. Spirituality can't be anything else than this.

Our love for shortcuts and defying order is one of our biggest weaknesses as human beings, especially in this generation. I am one person who doesn't like to be confined or limited in my operations but in my trying to think and operate outside the box I make sure I shouldn't go against the principles that govern the universe. These principles bring true and lasting success.

The Difference Between Spirituality and Religion
I want to dissect a little into these two areas that are separated by a very thin line. Usually, a religious man

thinks he is spiritual. Religion in today's context is more of claiming to believe in the spiritual yet all you do is go to church or mosque or a temple without the actual spiritual connection with spiritual forces. In every faith, if the being you are worshipping doesn't show up in any way when you seek that being the right way, then what you are seeking doesn't exist.

Dictionary gave one of the closest definitions of religion in line with what I want to explain about religion. It says it's the feeling or expression of human love, fear, or awe of some superhuman and overruling power, whether by profession of belief, **by the observance of rites and ceremonies,** or by the conduct of life. Spirituality is about seeking to understand the spiritual being you claim to worship and serve.

It's not about observing the man-made rituals, programs and activities but the desire and pursuit to get acquainted with the realities of the spiritual realm and having a relationship with whom you are worshipping if he or she truly exists. Spirituality is about allowing the principles of your faith to assimilate into your being. It's about holding on to your faith dearly from pure understanding.

This is the reason I said that though the purpose may be the reason for building a structure or institution – your life, spirituality is the foundation and skeleton that hold that structure together – tt brings sanity and integrity to your life and achievement just as values do to an institution. How good your spiritual stand is, determines how high, wide and strong you can be to handle things in your life.

Spirituality ideally determines your core values, character development or formation, world view and the basis of your governing principles. In the end, these determine how high you can rise, how much you can support, the challenges you can handle and how long you can stay standing. It also provides stabilizers to your soul such as peace, hope, joy among other things which helps you to think straight, remain positive and keep on believing.

It is necessary that you base your life on stable things which can't be influenced by outside circumstances. Learn to define your life by things or principles that are constant and don't disappoint. The only way you can have peace and joy regardless of your circumstances is when the source is constant. The only way you can be a person with integrity, unconditional love and caring is when that which drives you doesn't change. Other than that, you become an unstable person who walks with the world tossed to and from like a floater by the waves in the sea. Dr Myles Munroe said that your faith, hope and peace is as strong as the source you base them on.

This is what Christianity (Christian Spirituality) should do or be to you if you are a Christian. It shouldn't be something you just observe rather assimilate its principles into your being. First and foremost, it should be who you are. The word should be life in you; the word and you should be one. It should be the basis of your character and decision making.

The Christian principles should be deeply embedded within you and act as a map or boundary to guide you side by side with your purpose as your compass. There is a reason the word of God is called life because you are meant to live and become it. You should become the word and live it, everything about you should ooze the word. That is Christian Spirituality.

The quality of one's Christianity is manifested in the quality of one's soul through character.
"Either make the tree good and the fruit good or make then tree corrupt and its fruit corrupt; for a tree is known by its fruit. Offspring of vipers, how are you able to speak good things, being evil? For out of the abundance of the heart the mouth speaks. The good man out of the good treasure of his heart brings out good things, and the wicked man out of the wicked treasure brings out wicked things." **Matthews 12:33-35 AFV**

Spirituality is about trying to make your mind aware of the spiritual realm, pushing to tap into the spiritual realm deliberately. Being aware of the spiritual forces and principles that govern the universe and align yourself to your advantage. It's not just about the knowledge but more so the experience of the reality of the truth you are learning. That is spirituality.

A spiritual man desires the truth and will stop at nothing until he gets it. To him church or Mosque or Temple belonging isn't enough, he desires connection with deity more. You need to question your faith and make it personal. It's your responsibility. To one who desires true spirituality, what man says to him or her doesn't matter unless it's in line with the principles of the truth he or she believes in. Despite learning the truth in his place of worship, he or she goes on a journey to search more of the truth on his or her own in the way it should be sought like the Berean Christians who searched in the Bible by themselves to see if what Apostle Paul was teaching was in line with the truth. Knowing how crucial their spirituality was, they left it in no man's hands. They believed in God and truth more than they had faith in men of God.

"The brothers immediately sent Paul and Silas away by night to Berea, and when they arrived, they went into the Jewish synagogue. Now, these Jews were more noble than those in Thessalonica; they received the word with all eagerness, examining the Scriptures daily to see if these things were so." **Acts 17:10-11**

For some, going to church, Mosque or Temple is enough even though nothing about their relationship with deity changes. I will say for Christian Faith and from my experience, God is real, He is not an idea and He seeks a relationship with you.

Up until you find God, you will struggle to meet your purpose. You may do a lot of good but that may not be your purpose.

The Misconception
People usually look at the word of God as if God is trying to control them on what they can or can't do in or with their lives. They can't be more wrong. Let me

show you something. Assume there is harmful radiation material on the road or someone with an infectious disease like COVID-19. Then some people have no idea about it and want to get into contact with such out of their ignorance. You choose to warn or notify them, out of love, of what lies ahead, and its effects over time.

Remember the effects of these dangers are seldom immediate. So, even those that didn't listen to your warning think nothing has happened to them. And the other group that listened to you out of trust (faith) see those who have just disobeyed you seeming unaffected, it becomes even harder for them to believe you next time. Worse still because the effects aren't immediate, it's hard to attribute them to the exposure due to time-length between the contact and effects. People still can't connect what is happening to them or someone to the warning they didn't heed someday.

In the short-term, there is usually no difference between these two groups because of what is known as the incubation period, the time between exposure and the beginning of effects of exposure in our lives. The fact that you can't see the effects yet doesn't mean it's not happening. A branch that has been detached from the main trunk doesn't show withering signs right away. So, from the example above the ones who believed you and avoided the exposure and eventual negative consequences even if they can't see it are called believers and those who don't, non-believers. That's how Christian Spirituality works.

You are either a believer in spiritual beings and principles or not. The fact that those that didn't believe don't have immediate effects prompts confusion in those that believed in you, and they are somewhat jealous of those that didn't believe in you as they seem to enjoy life by doing whatever they want. This was the exact experience of King David at some point but...

"Truly God is good to Israel, to those who are pure in heart. But as for me, my feet had almost stumbled, my steps had nearly slipped. For I was envious of the arrogant when I saw the prosperity of the wicked. For they have no pangs until death; their bodies are fat and sleek. They are not in trouble as others are; they are not stricken like the rest of mankind. Therefore, pride is their necklace; violence covers them as a garment. Their eyes swell out through fatness, their hearts overflow with follies. They scoff and speak with malice; loftily they threaten oppression. They set their mouths against the heavens and their tongue struts through the earth. Therefore, his people turn back to them and find no fault in them. And they say, "How can God know? Is there knowledge in the Most High?" Behold, these are the wicked; always at ease, they increase in riches. All in vain have I kept my heart clean and washed my hands in innocence. For all the day long I have been stricken and rebuked every morning. If I had said, "I will speak thus," I would have betrayed the generation of your children.

But when I thought how to understand this, it seemed to me a wearisome task, until I went into the sanctuary of

God; then I discerned their end. Truly you set them in slippery places; you make them fall to ruin. How they are destroyed in a moment, swept away utterly by terrors ! Like a dream when one awakes, O Lord , when you rouse yourself, you despise them as phantoms. When my soul was embittered, when I was pricked in heart, I was brutish and ignorant ; I was like a beast toward you . Nevertheless, I am continually with you; you hold my right hand . You guide me with your counsel, and afterward, you will receive me to glory ." Psalms 73:1-21 ESV

This is a perfect summary from King David about the course of life. God is not there to control us but rather guide us out of love for His creation. He is the one who created the universe and set in motion the governing principles and their consequences.

So, the Creator of the universe put governing principles to the universe that even those that don't believe in His existence yet obey or observe the principles benefit from them just as the sun shines on everyone. Most of these principles don't make sense to our natural minds because they don't follow the pattern of physical principles.

Some people use these principles without realizing they are the principles that govern the universe. People like Bill and Melinda Gates help the poor, and they grow in wealth and fame, and people wonder how and why? Giving and making a difference to people is obedience to a spiritual principle which unlocks spiritual blessings whether you are a Christian or not.

Everyone who applies those principles coupled with the principle of faith, as opposed to doubt and fear, bears results. Of what benefit is Christianity then if these principles can apply to everyone? Salvation, blessings, grace and power which give life hope, and make it and the work therein bearable.

In addition to that, Christianity helps you sustain your success because sustenance of your success is easy when you continue in the principles which is hard for most non-believers. That's why the Bible says that a wicked man gathers wealth for the righteous man (Proverbs 13:22; Ecclesiastes 2:26). Christian success since it's based on pure Christian Principles it adds no sorrow.

"The blessing of the LORD makes rich, and he adds no sorrow with it." **Proverbs 10:22**

Spiritual principles bow down or bend to no man's wishes. Just as the principle of friction which if you don't obey you suffer the consequences. Whether you know it or believe in it doesn't matter because they are in operation. Though you may choose to be ignorant of them, it doesn't mean you won't be affected. On the other hand, if there are good spiritual principles which you could ride on and benefit from, but you choose to be ignorant of and not apply them, you suffer loss. Ignorance is never an excuse.

The Composition of Man
You are a spirit being with a soul and living in a

physical body. In other words, you are housed in that physical body; you are not the body rather the being who lives in it. The body just gives you the ability to be relevant on earth and interact with the physical environment.

The fact that we can't see the spirit and the soul of a man doesn't mean they are not there. There have been testimonies of people in near-death experiences who claimed to have moved out of their bodies. What moved out? Just as we can't see the wind, rather its effects, all we see about the spirit and the soul of man are the character, decisions and the actions that the body takes. What your body does is just a manifestation of how your spirit and soul is. If we were to transplant your spirit and soul into another body, then that body will behave as your previous body did because the body does what the spirit and the soul command.

The reason a physically challenged or disabled person is no less of a human being is the fact that we are not the body but the one carried therein. They are complete spirits with complete souls. Do you ever wonder where new ideas or inventions that one has never seen or heard of come from? Do they come from your mind? Do you retain them from memory?

Napoleon Hill in his book, "Think and Grow Rich", brought in a great argument about imagination which will ease my work in bringing forth my argument. He said that there are two kinds of imagination: The Synthetic Imagination and Creative Imagination.

He continued to say that synthetic imagination arranges or re-arranges old concepts, ideas or plans into new combinations to come up with a new thing. It doesn't create something new from out of the blues but rather uses the work of experience, education and observation with which the mind is fed.

On the other hand, the Creative Imagination is the ability to tap into the Infinite Intelligence (The spiritual realm) that makes you have a new idea out of nothing. Which means a person can tap into a greater network of knowledge and wisdom from the realm of the unknown by some means.

I am here to clarify further that your soul is the one that is involved in Synthetic Imagination whilst your Spirit is the one that enables you to have the Creative Imagination. Ideas never come out of the blues, they are sourced somewhere, and the tools of sourcing them differ.

The Bible says that the things we see come from the things that already exist in the spirit but can't capture with our senses.

"Because of our faith, we know that the world was made at God's command. We also know that what can be seen was made out of what cannot be seen." **Hebrews 11:3 CEV**

The challenge that we usually have is the lack of knowledge or skill to grasp what our spirits can capture in the spiritual realm. Others call the spirit the subconscious mind with respect to the conscious mind. One of the main ways to tap from the subconscious mind is through deep meditation.

Meditation helps you tap into your spirit and download new ideas from the realm of the unknown. This is the reason people that meditate over a problem, or generally that meditate end up having solutions or new inventions, peace etc because these are available abundantly in our spirits from the spiritual realm. Some apply this technique, but they just don't know that they had access into their spirits.

Let me lay down some piece of scripture that put across this idea better.

1 Corinthians 2:9-12 "But, as it is written, What no eye has seen, nor ear heard, nor the heart of man imagined that God has prepared for those who love him"— these things God has revealed to us through the Spirit. For the Spirit searches everything, even the depths of God. For who knows a person's thoughts except the spirit of that person, which is in him? So also no one comprehends the thoughts of God except the Spirit of God. Now we have received not the spirit of the world, but the Spirit who is from God, that we might understand the things freely given us by God."

The Bible also says that believers are one with God's Spirit which means whatever the Spirit of God has access to, the spirit of man, that is connected to His

Spirit, also has access to the same. The challenge now is for man's soul through the mind to have access to the unlimited resources his spirit can access. This is where prophets from both evil and good come from, they are just people who have mastered the art of making sense of what their spirits have access to in the spirit. Meditation will help you with that.

"But he who is joined to the Lord becomes one spirit with Him." **1 Corinthians 6:17**

The soul consists of the mind, the will and the emotions whilst the spirit contains the conscience and new ideas.

The Void in Man's Soul

There is a void in man's soul which for ages people have tried to fill in with all sorts of things but to no avail. Others think it's education, status quo, good looks, fame, knowledge, etc but all these have been found wanting. Even though the euphoria from achieving those things temporarily covers the top of the hole, it always reappears.

That's why the preacher in Ecclesiastes said everything done from the fleshly desires is vanity (Ecclesiastes 1:14). It's like filling a hole with chaff, and you test it with the fire of time to test the quality of the material only to realize that it's burnt out in a few weeks to months. This is what time does to the achievements with which we try to fill the void. In a few days or months, you realize you still have that emptiness.

I can challenge you that if you feel this void and you can't fill it with anything else, try Jesus. He knows how to fill it beyond your satisfaction. Pursue Him according to the principles of Christianity: faith, desire, patience and expectation, and see what happens to that void. Your soul through the sixth sense (spirit) tells you of your emptiness and the desire to fill the void. When you eventually invite Jesus to fill it, you know it has been filled because you can't feel it anymore, as long as you remain in a good relationship with Him.

"The Spirit Himself bears witness with our spirit that we are children of God." **Romans 8:16**

The void you feel is a way of your subconscious mind telling you that it's starved of something. So, the more you continue feeding it earthly food, success and information, it can't be filled because the hunger is spiritual not physical or from the soul.

Nothing else except Jesus has worked for people, that I know, who have successfully filled this hole of emptiness. This is not a trick, try it. You will realize nothing in this life is more fulfilling than having Him fill that void every day.

Spiritual Realm and Forces

If men are spirits, there should be a spiritual realm out there.

Contrary to what some people think, I don't believe in spiritual beings or forces just because I have been brainwashed. I believe in them because I have experienced their effects. Quickly, let me narrate to you some of the things I experienced when I engaged in the spiritual realm or forces, which people claim don't exist. I will not talk about being touched by the power of God which most don't believe anyway. Whether you believe in them or not it's all up to you. All these things happened when I was in college.

In my first year, I went for a night of prayer and one of my prayer petitions was that God should help my roommate and I have a cleanroom. I had tried so hard in my power to have it clean after I heard that cleanliness is next to godliness but to no avail. Our bad habits let us down. I thought of taking it up to the spiritual force (God) for whatever help he would offer in His infinite power when I remembered that He is all able.

At this time, my roommate was back at school since he didn't make it to the night of prayer. I prayed that God should help us make our room clean since our habits failed us. When I came back to school in the morning and entered our room, I found my roommate's side cleaned up and neat.

I wondered what had happened, and even before I asked him about it, he said that when he was going to bed the previous night, he saw everything as normal but when he woke up the next morning, he realized that the room was in a mess, so he had to clean it up. I was dumbfounded. I laughed out loudly in disbelief, and when he asked why I was laughing, I told him I would explain to him later.

This reminded me of the story of Mordecai in the book of Esther. A night before Mordecai's execution, the king had to remember the favour that Mordecai did for him, which he had not repaid. Of all days, the king had to be troubled a night before the execution (Esther 5 and 6). Once again, the spiritual forces intervened and troubled him to search for something he couldn't before.

The second time was when a group of senior students went to party in our prayer room (Spiritual Lounge at Malawi College of Medicine). My brother in the Lord, now Pr. Aggrey Phiri and I were infuriated by this act and we confronted them. They took the braii stand outside the lounge but left their extension connected to the socket inside the lounge with their sound system loudly playing outside.

Our spirits were vexed, we prayed whilst moving around the extension that was left inside. I wanted something to happen, but I wasn't clear on what exactly. I just wanted these people to respect the place as we did. Maybe I just wanted God to show His power by showing up in some way. I was amazed at what happened next. There was a power surge (just in the room and nowhere else) which caused the extension's plug to burn and got stuck to the socket on the wall, the PA system outside got burnt as well. Surprisingly, the lights weren't affected. Almost three guys came in and tried to take out the plug from the socket, but it couldn't come out.

Once again, it showed me that the spiritual forces and realm are real. This is aside from the power that rushes through me when I have a touch from the spirit of God or men of God. The spiritual forces work for those who believe before they see to experience. Spiritual principles don't and can't bend just for you, you should align yourself to them to work. They are what they are and can't act otherwise just to prove a point to you.

People want the spiritual forces to reveal themselves when they don't believe in them, that's not how it works. They are not like a human being who wants to prove you wrong when you challenge them otherwise. You need to speak their language and observe their principles, then and only then will you see them in operation in your life.

The Advantage of Being Spiritual
As I have said earlier, a spiritual man is one that has awareness of spiritual happenings and can take advantage of it to influence the physical happening. The spiritual influences the physical whilst the actions we do in the physical has a bearing on whether the spiritual forces intervene in our affairs or not.

There are both good and evil spiritual forces. They both can help you influence physical happenings with their prices to pay. Your physical manifestations reveal the kind of spiritual force and the level of connection you have with it. It shows how much access you have from them and how much influence they have on your soul.

Have you ever encountered or heard a story of a small child or old person, in an African setting, threatening a physically big and strong person that they will deal with? Do you wonder where they get their confidence and boldness from? Usually, they are not bluffing because they know, though they may be physically weak, they yet have the power to influence spiritual forces that control the physical happenings.

People can foretell times or events according to the spiritual forces they are connected to. I have heard of witch-doctors who can tell people events in their lives, exactly how they have happened and why they are happening by tapping into the spiritual realm. I have heard of men of God who can tell people what is happening in their lives not because they have stalked the person or had someone tell them something about the person. They can also tell people what will happen - prophecy, and things happen. I have had moments where people tell me stories about and omit their names and I automatically get their names.

I believe what people call déjà vu is you experien-cing what your spirit foresaw only that you couldn't remember it. Or the moments people dream about things and they end up happening. I ever had such a dream where things unfolded before me. Science will try to make sense of these things, but the truth is that most of them are just beyond science.

These spiritual connections have even the power to

change and transform your character from within. This is what happened to me when I got born again. Over time I got good characters which I can't explain how I got them. Suddenly, I had love, joy, peace and hope beyond measure in my life. My peace, love and joy have never been about what I am going through, feels like it's just part of me, my nature. No matter how much I am hurt, I don't stop loving. My work-mates usually wonder the level of peace and the confidence I have even amidst the storm at work. It's not something I force myself to do consciously, it's who I am. I am not saying, I am perfect, but I am far better than I used to be.

What you need to translate spiritual things into physical counterparts is through words and acts of faith (belief in with action). Words you speak materialize the spiritual things you see in your mind's eye and believe in. According to your level of faith, and usually, this translation is not instant, it happens over time. This is the reason, psychologists and motivational speakers say we become what we obsess about. The reason is what we obsess about we think about, we talk about and we believe in.

The same principle that is applied in self-talk to become someone, works for things you want to possess as well. It won't be instant. Believe, confess it and keep on believing then you will see it. You will have ideas on how to have it, people will appear to help you have it and doors will open for you to enter and get it. People in the world apply this principle only that they don't know what they are applying. It causes things to rearrange sooner or later into what we believe they should be, in career, business, relationships, etc.

Faith or belief taps into the Infinite Power (spiritual realm) that controls nature. That's why for those people that set their goals and strongly believe in them eventually have resource provisions to realize their goals. Faith is the power of attraction that motivation speakers talk about.

Things start rearranging by themselves, people they need come their way and doors they need to enter present themselves. We create in our minds and with words of faith and continued belief things are formed or arranged according to our belief.

Challenges to Believing the Spiritual

It's not easy for one to believe in the spiritual realm or spiritual forces influencing lives or circumstances on earth, let alone for a man of science because he can't prove them. To a man of science, things he can't capture by his 5 senses don't exist.

Throughout history, you will find out that there are two main things that man has desired so much and they are freedom and power to control. Dr Myles Munroe in most of his books on Kingdom Series and Potential repeatedly said, which I find to be true, that people don't want to be controlled or be told what to do but they either want to have the power to control not only themselves but also their environment or circumstances. Both the forces of good and evil promise control but consequences differ.

Man wants God to think like him whilst God wants man to upgrade his thinking and operations to His level.

Spiritual things do not make sense to the natural mind initially but as you allow it to sink in, it starts to make sense. You should forget principles of science which demands proof first and states that seeing is believing and go by the spiritual principle of faith which is contrary and says believe to see (John 11:40).

"The natural person does not accept the things of the Spirit of God, for they are folly to him, and he is not able to understand them because they are spiritually discerned." **Corinthians 2:14**

People tend to fear or resist spiritual things because of three main reasons:

1. Ignorance to the truth, and close mindedness.

2. Fear of losing the quo as the new thing may out-date them since it operates on new principles which they are not familiar with, hence risking being under the leadership of those who understand them, "no-bodies".

3. people are afraid of the thought of someone or some being having control over their lives – they don't like to surrender and put their fate in the hands of an unknown being.

They think they will leave life to chance when they

believe in a greater power, and they will never be in control of their lives. They feel like they will lose their autonomy, but they can't be more wrong. The more spiritual you are the more you are in control not only of your own life but circumstances around you. The Bible has been misinterpreted big time.

The fact that people don't understand the topic of spirituality unless one desires to, they are quick to dismiss it as superstition. Or they feel like believing in the spiritual nullifies science, very wrong. Spirituality is an upgrade science can't explain.

King Solomon was a spiritual man yet through spirituality he explained the trees, the beast, reptiles, etc. God gave him the wisdom to understand nature which is science yet without experimenting on them. A spiritual man just knows things as they are (what is called a hunch), science comes behind to prove those things.

You can't afford to be unspiritual in this life, because life is spiritual. Everything that has worked for you this far is because you have believed in and applied spiritual principles that have the ultimate influence over life.

✦ CHARACTER DEPARTMENT

Chapter Fourteen

"The Character Ethic taught that there are basic principles of effective living and that people can only experience true success and enduring happiness as they learn and integrate these principles into their basic character."
Steven R. Covey

Character is a word from which characteristics comes from. Character talks about the inherent nature of something not only the physical outlook but also the material of make and the behavioural patterns. For you as a person it goes deep into the soul, and looks at how you think, operate and interact with others. It goes hand in hand with identity; your identity determines who you are and how you operate and how you operate reveals or gives you an identity to the world around you. That's why being a Christian is not about who you claim to be but the manifestation of the new creature you claim to be (1 Timothy 2:19; Matthews 3:7-10; 2 Corinthian 5:17-18).

In this motivation speaker generation, rarely do they speak about character development but rather personality development. In other words, they don't focus on the intrinsic good you should be that determines what you can or can't do naturally, but rather focus on what you should be doing or how you should do it to get or achieve something. They are more focused on quick fixes; how to make things happen in no time, how to convince, influence, win or control people. I may say, we are in a "How To Do" generation as opposed to "How To Be". We need to focus on being more than doing. As earlier said, who or what we are determines what we can do. *"Do less, be more."* – Elizabeth Grace Saunders, Author.

Character is deep and is the source of true and sustainable personality traits and habits. It anchors them. You must force yourself to maintain a good personality when you have a bad character because you have to be conscious to pretend all the time. There is an African proverb which says that character is like pregnancy, you can never hide it; sooner or later, like pregnancy, it comes out in the open.

Character helps with the motives and intentions of your actions. Character causes you to be pure at heart; you don't have to worry about anything because your actions have the purest of intentions when done. You don't have to look over your shoulder because you did something wrong. Character guards your actions.

Some of the good character traits that you should be developing from your spirit to your soul include integrity, humility, modesty, self-esteem, courage, hardworking,

compassion, selflessness, love, meekness, gentleness, joyousness, peacefulness, patience, endurance, etc. If you look carefully at them, you will realize that they are all fruits of the Holy Spirit (Galatians 5:22-23) and that tells you how deep and fundamental Christian Principles are to a human soul.

Importance of Good Character

The true test of character comes with time. In times of testing, our true self tends to emerge. A true character has a habit of showing up at such moments. When you have a good character, you remain on course-though momentary deviation may occur in a moment of weakness.

Good Character doesn't only help you to attain success the right way but also helps you to sustain that success. Good character aids you to the top. Bad character, however, does exactly the opposite. I believe you know people who made a fortune or got a job or a network of customers and lost it sooner than anticipated because of their character.

I have heard a couple of stories about makeup artists who lost their customers because of their moods, personalities and attitudes. Don't take character for granted, it determines whether you can stay on top or not. People have been fired or missed promotions because of bad characters. Why should bosses promote you to a more influential position when everything about you screams against the core values of the organization?

Good character opens doors for you because it helps you stand the test of time when it comes to areas of integrity. One can only pretend for so long. Good character guards your manners and you are a person who can't just bend your values to fit someone or something because it's not in you to do so. You don't pretend to be something that you are not. You stand true to values and embrace who you are. With good character your actions are safeguarded, you can't just do anything anyhow, you are automatically more careful.

It helps you with the way you look at, perceive and interpret the world around you. No one sees the world as it is, we see it according to who we are. This determines how you behave and interact with people, and that comes out genuinely and naturally. You don't have to force it or to be deliberately conscious to maintain consistency in certain behaviour. It's already who you are; you don't act out of false pretence of personality.

When the going gets tough, when all the techniques and skills have fallen apart, it is character that defines who is who in every area of life. It is the last line of defence.

The storms of life come to shake us, but it is only those that are truly built-in character, through sound principles, that stand the tests even the great test of time. Discipline, persistence, determination and grit among others are part of good character, and you can't do anything worthwhile without these.

People change for the worse in behaviour (personality) when they come across fame, wealth and change in status because they never developed their character in the first place. We are so obsessed with success, yet we are not preparing ourselves on how we will handle it when it finally comes. Character is what protects you from negative influences in the environment. It helps you to keep your head in the game and keep you sober from the intoxication of success; you have success, but success doesn't have you.

I believe people partly get into addictions of smoking, drunkenness, using recreational drugs due to lack of character. Character helps you diffuse the bombs and darts of frustration life throws at you. It is the fountain of a positive attitude. You embrace challenges and setbacks as part of life and as things that you need to pass through to get better. You know you have the ability within you to go past such hardship without the use of any substance that promises a quick fix to the current storm. Instead of postponing them to a later time, you face them head-on now and find solutions to them.

Drinking or using drugs to drown your sorrows or get high is a sign of weakness in character and lack of internal measures or ability (good characters) to handle or diffuse frustration from denial, rejection, failure, loss or betrayal. When you have a good character, you can create your own happiness from within or from things that don't threaten your well-being eventually.

How Do You Attain Good Character?
"It is, basically, the story of one man's effort to integrate

certain principles and habits deep within his nature."
Steven R. Covey - 7 Habits of Highly Effective People

Character is built through internalizing sound principles and values to make them part of your nature. It's a process of unlearning old and wrong principles and learning new ones. You should stop focusing on the quick fixes in your personality. Don't focus on the skills and charisma before intentions at your core.

The good that you want to speak and behave should start from your core, who you are. You should be naturally good with no ill intentions. It's a matter of putting your intentions right. Comes easy with Christian Spirituality as well, from my experience.

Recognize that it's possible to develop a new character. You need to start watching your intentions when doing things and start correcting yourself. There is a third person in you who can watch your actions and remind you from the outside. Use him or her. The one you call the good side of you. Life is fun and fulfilling this way.

LEADERSHIP AND MANAGEMENT DEPARTMENT

Chapter Fifteen

Leaders are in short supply in this world. One principle that I have discovered in life is that you can't master something in a larger setting which you can't in a smaller setting. We usually think leadership is about having a position and leading others or managing things; to the contrary, the highest level of leadership is to self.

God created man to be a leader not only when it comes to other people but more so to self. How we handle ourselves shows whether we are good self-leaders or not. How your life turns out to be is dependent on how good you are as a self-leader; how you lead yourself through the decisions you make and the actions you take to beat procrastination. Whether we are successful or not, it reveals the quality of our self-leadership.

How you handle your life, your body, your feelings and desires show whether you are in control or you are being led by things you were meant to lead and keep in check. Maturity is not measured in years lived or the size of the body rather through self-responsibility which is self-leadership and management.

Since your life is a project and just like any project, it needs a leader and or a manager to guide and manage it. Since life is a journey it needs a tour guide. You can't leave your life project and journey in the hands of anyone else because first, they don't know who you should be and where you are going and second, rarely do people have the best interest of others at heart. The journey of growth is not only one of independence but more so on assuming responsibility for self. Desiring independence is desiring self -leadership which most African nations are failing at.

The self-control, courage, self-esteem, self-love, self-discipline, integrity, good morals are part of self - leadership. How good you are at those things reflect when you assume leadership over others.

If you let your feelings and desires tell you what you can and can't do, then you will be a slave of your own body and unproductive in this life. For you to be productive you need to do what needs to be done which the body is usually against. Self -leadership is mastery over your body, knowing who you should be, where you are going or should be going, the resources needed for your journey or project and laying out a plan and strategies on how to finish that project or travel that journey to the end. If you

can do this in your own life, then you can also do it in other people's lives; without that, you are not fit.

I believe, we get to be drug, sex and alcohol addicts and procrastinators because we can't keep our bodies under. We let our bodies lead and we follow. We entertained wrong desires which became habits and addictions. Now, we can't tell our bodies what to not do; we can't help but feed our bodies whatever they desire. Whatever addiction you may have just shows how poor you have been at self-leadership in that area.

Not everyone gets to be a virgin at 30 years because they never had opportunities or don't have feelings but because they can control their feelings. Addicts quit alcohol, sleeping around and drugs not because they no longer have the desire but because they rise and start exercising their leadership responsibilities and take back control over their own lives.

Your life will never move forward, or you can't achieve anything in life until you grow to a level that you can keep your body under and do what you should do when you need to. That is leadership! There is no successful man in this life who never could self -lead and do what's necessary. That's why Plato said, *"For (a) man to conquer himself is the first and noblest of all victories... The first and greatest victory is to conquer yourself; to be conquered by yourself is of all things most shameful and vile."*

If you can't control or direct your own life, can't control your feelings, desires and procrastination among other things, why should you be trusted to lead on a larger scale? Is it because there is money involved then you will be a man of integrity and you won't procrastinate? I think not. If you have personal leadership flaws the same manifest when you take up other posts because it's who you are. Learn to lead your life in the direction you would want to go and attain those goals before you jump into wanting to lead others towards certain goals.

You are the only one who can get you to your destination because you are the only one who knows it well. If you can't lead yourself then you will never get to your destination. If you want to be successful in life and meet all the dreams you have, you need to work out self-leadership and direct your body on what it should or shouldn't be doing per the need at the time. Without that then dreaming and wishing will be your only achievement in this life. You can't be anything without leadership knowledge, skills and abilities.

You should be able to lead yourself into things that matter to your purpose knowing that you won't live on earth for eternity. Knowing how to spend your time and money for maximum impact on your purpose requires self - leadership and management skills.

You will always need some level of leadership in your relationship, family, workplace, business, friendship for you to be successful in those areas. This is how vitally important leadership is. You can't get promoted at work without leading some people under you. You can't have a successful family without leadership skills to lead your children and spouse if you are a man. Women usually prefer men with leadership characteristics.

Every successful businessperson or entrepreneur

needs leadership skills; they should lead their business idea to success. They may also have employees they need to lead and manage.

Following your body's demands, even if you are housed in it, it's like following the people you should be leading. Wake up and take up that self -leadership role as you work on your life project and lead yourself to your destination.

Chapter Sixteen

"All things that are lawful are permitted to me, but not all things that are permitted are profitable. All things that are lawful are permitted to me, but all things that are permitted do not edify." **1 Corinthians 10:23 AFV**

Education or the learning system is one of the essential systems that must be functional in every person if he or she wants to amount to anything in life. Within each one of us is the potential to learn how to learn which we should desire to harness. And in us, there is potential to become and do things which can only be unlocked through learning new information and skills. Life is about growth and development and these come through learning and application of that knowledge.

In simple terms, learning is the ability to understand or capture information or skills into one's mind for application. Wisdom is the ability to apply the knowledge and skills that we have learnt the right way, whilst foolishness is the opposite which is acting against the information you have. That's why we have educated fools, people who have the information yet behave otherwise. They are intelligent yet foolish. Intelligence is your ability to learn. That's where IQ comes from. High IQ guarantees intelligence but not wisdom. That's why we have brilliant doctors who are obese (with no efforts to lose weight), drunkards and chain smokers yet know well thier negative effects over time.

You can only be who you should be through learning and training. Any transformation that you can ever desire both in primary and secondary areas of life, and every achievement you can ever attain lies in learning.

Even though other people take part in building your life, you are the master builder, and for you direct them on how to help you build your life, you must first learn how. You should know the needed resource and how much it will cost to complete building yourself and taking a journey to your destination, and how to raise those resources.

Ask those who look like your future-version to teach you how they got where they are. Learn about the cost, sacrifices to be made and challenges to be met and overcome along the way. Equip yourself for the future.
You never know what you have or don't have until you learn about it. Sometimes you don't know that you are lacking in some way until you learn that you do.

If you want to be successful in life, then you shouldn't shy away from acquiring new knowledge and skills. You should be a person who desires to learn all the time regardless of who is teaching you. You must develop that desire and ability to learn. Grow and develop from where you are to the next level which can only happen through learning.

After you find out your identity and purpose the next thing is to learn how to become the person who you should be and push on becoming that person till you are ready to fulfil your purpose. It doesn't matter where you are starting from now, but if you start learning towards the right direction that's all that matters. Acquire that needed information and skills to be ready for that assignment and be ready to handle every area of your life.

Formal education is not all there is. There is more to learn from informal education than the formal. Aside from expanding your thinking abilities, formal education will only teach you mainly one area of your life which is a profession. Other than that, the rest of your life depends on informal education from different people. You can even have informal education right within formal education.

Methods of Learning

There are two styles or methods of learning and acquiring information which I will define according to this book: active and passive learning. I'll use these words loosely due to the lack of better words. Focus on the ideas, not the labelling.

Passive learning is when someone is feeding you information on a topic or topics, and you don't engage with them through questions. This is very common in formal education where rarely students engage their teachers with questions to learn more. It also happens from books where you can read without questioning or getting more answers from people or other books. Students are not inquisitive to learn more. You take things as they come. This is not a very effective form of learning because it doesn't stimulate growth.

Active learning, on the other hand, is centred on you and you make it personal regardless of how many people are teaching or learning. Mostly you don't always wait for a teacher because due to your hunger to learn and grow, you search for one. You need to find people that can teach you and engage them to know more. Above all else develop a culture of active learning from things and processes around you.

When you can learn actively, you can use books, podcasts, pre-recorded lessons, journals, magazines, internet, movies, people around you, etc. You are a person who draws lessons from anything around you whether it has an intention to teach you or not.

You can learn from anyone if you are meek and hungry enough for new knowledge or skills. You can learn from your parents, friends, teachers, mentors, siblings, etc only if you are willing. You need to find mentors that have gone before you and dig out knowledge and wisdom from them.

to write down any lesson you learn each day. You can learn and write down lessons as you learn, or you can write them down as you retire to bed and reflect on the day. Learn to write things down when someone is teaching you, it helps you with active listening and reminding you of the information after some time.

Either way, you need to be a person that is hungry to learn new information and skills because that's the only way you can get better and well equipped to meet your purpose. Keep on building on the knowledge that you currently have, the more you learn the easier it becomes to learn new things. Mind you, learning is not an end it's rather a means to an end which is being better and wiser. Remember knowledge is not power "Actionable, practical or applied knowledge" is power. New knowledge is useless if you don't apply it. Don't be like the graduates who have papers yet have nothing to show for at their workplace.

There are 2 things that we learn and that is information and skills, and they can be learnt both actively and passively. We need both along our journey.

What Do We Learn?
When you look back at the opening scripture you will realize that not everything good is right for you. Not everything good that people learn out there, you should be learning. You may have the ability to learn anything in life, but life is too short to learn everything. Use your self-leadership skills and tailor your education to the knowledge and skills that will help you make an impact in this life through your purpose, vision and mission.

Set for yourself objectives that will help you get closer to becoming the person you should be and meeting your purpose. Acquire knowledge and skills that are tailored to your journey so that you live an effective life and walk a worthy journey. Let learning and education be centred on your needs. If you don't know who you should develop into and where you are going, you think any education opportunity is yours. Let not the world dictate for you what you should learn but according to your purpose, vision and mission, decide what is right for you.

🌿 FINANCIAL DEPARTMENT

Chapter Seventeen

"The more money works for you, the less you have to work for money." **Idowu Koyenikan**

"Money is only a tool. It will take you wherever you wish, but it will not (or shouldn't) replace you as the driver." **Ayn Rand**

After laying up a foundation for your life, let me take you through another vital area of your life. This is the area of finance. Every project needs money and so does every journey to a distant destination. King Solomon said that money answers all things (Ecclesiastes 10:19). Though it might not be entirely true money is indeed a solution to many things. It would be a great injustice on my part to negligibly exclude skills that enable one to grow financially as they discover and live out their purposes.

Financial systems can be summed up into two arms: money making and money management.

Money Making Skills

Career (job employment) is good. It is, however, not the only way one can get money. We often allow life to place us in a box and determine what we can and cannot do through formal education. When a person has not received a formal education, we are quick to conclude that is the end for them. Perhaps we cannot blame such a thought considering the systems at play. Yet to assume that such a person has hit the end of the road is perhaps an oversight. Our brains are creative. We often forget this. When push comes to shove, we can think our way into methods and ways of generating money outside of the formal employment arena. We just have to use the brain.

There are great names in American history: Henry Ford, Thomas. E. Edison, Bill Gates and Steve Jobs whose formal education was cut short. Now, what about Malawi? Eston Muli and Godfrey Masauli both did not have a formal education initially. What about William Kamkwamba? The boy (now a man) who harnessed the wind (with now a feature film). Money making has little to do with formal education. That's how much we have been brainwashed to the point that we get jealous and angry when those that are not formally educated or have lesser education either earn more or employ us to work for them.

We just must come to our senses that money-making is never about the level of formal career education but rather how you resonate with principles of success when it comes to money-making. All you need from formal education is just basic mathematics and a little language to learn how to read and write so that you can learn money-making skills. Money making is an art with its own set of knowledge,

mentality and skills on how to attract money through

seeing opportunities, creating value, marketing it and making the sale.

There are several ways of earning money; some are honourable whilst others aren't. These money-making methods include stealing, begging, gambling, working, borrowing, doing legal or illegal business or investing in other 's endeavours. All these methods, including stealing-for-hire, are about creating value and getting others to see and pay for it.

Beggars sell ideas to get sympathy. Scammers sell ideas to prey on people. An employee sells knowledge and skills. Borrowers sell stories and circumstances. Business schemes sell products and services. Investors sell money. All you should realize is that the success in earning money through any of those areas depends on your level of knowledge and skills in them. Each of them requires their mentality and skills for you to succeed in money-making. Being good in your primary area of work does not automatically mean you will be good at business or any other area. Being good in your primary area of business does not automatically equate to you being good at a particular profession. It is a learning process for everyone.

Stealing
For those that successfully steal from institutions and homes have developed knowledge and skills for them not to be caught (though sooner or later get caught or exposed). Someone else may try to steal from the same company or area but get caught. Why? Because they lack the skills and knowledge for not getting

caught. We have heard stories of people who tried to steal from their offices and were caught in a matter of days whilst others were not discovered till after years. Even stealing through trickery which requires one to be well versed in its craft.

Gambling and Betting

Gambling to most of us seems like a game of chance. Yet to those that understand it they are happy to play. I have a friend who makes money from gambling. I however cannot. I don't think it is healthy and safe. I think it easily leads to addiction. But those who learn how to make money through this means do so to their fortune (or misfortune).

Betting, even though it seems random and very much a game of chance, is not a game of chance. The main challenge to betting is betting to win more which usually you have to bet against the odds.

At present (EPL 2019/2020 season), Liverpool has more chances to beat Norwich City. If you follow English Premier League football then you're going to bet for Liverpool unless if you want to bet against the odds. Even in horse racing, you have to go for the history of the horse race and know which ones have won in the past and you bet on them. So even in betting, you have to have the knowledge and the skill (wisdom) to know when to bet or not. to beat Fulham United, you will.

Begging

For someone to beg and be given money, also requires special knowledge and skills. It's not easy for someone to pull out their hard-earned money and give you just like that. It even requires a strong mentality to withstand what people would say about you. Imagine going outside to beg from those who know you. What would they say about you?

People bring in every possible trick to successfully earn money through begging. Just as in business they sell you their ideas and conditions to gain a level of sympathy. Their physical appearance and stature play a part in depicting the message of hardship. I saw a video on WhatsApp of an Indian man caught by police for pretending to be a cripple not only to beg but more so to convince people to give him money.

I heard a story of a young man who started his car hire business from alms. He wasn't a cripple. He was a guy from Blantyre Township. Even though I commend what he did with the money he managed to raise, my focus now is on the mental preparedness he had to go through and the patience he had to have for him to make money still. He is no longer begging now, and he has his businesses from the capital he raised.

Business

Some people jump into business and investment as a means for money-making without first acquiring the necessary mentality, knowledge and skills. They end up labelling business as too risky after they lose money due to their lack of preparedness. Even in electrical engineering, you know that the more knowledge you have the more you know where or where not to touch or step on to avoid being electrocuted. It's the same thing with business, the lesser the financial IQ the higher you are at risk of losing your money.

You can't get into business without first learning what that business is all about. It requires you to understand your service or product, challenges, competition and your market. You also need to develop a business mentality for you to withstand setbacks, losses and challenges that are in business. Why should you be good at something that you haven't invested in? We get out as much as we put in. You don't expect to just wake up one day and you are a doctor and know it all. It takes years of devouring knowledge and skills acquisition to not kill a patient. The more you learn about medicine the lower the risks of killing a patient due to mismanagement.

Investment

This is when you put money into other people's money. You give capital to people to do businesses and give you interest from your money. These include paper assets (bonds, shares) and money lending.

For you to make money out of this, knowledge and skills are equally required. People invest in bonds and shares and end up losing money because they have no idea about what is happening. Those that understand and have the skill to study the market trends know when and where to invest. Even when investing in people's business you should know what would work and what wouldn't.

Formal Education and Employment

It is possible to have people who have acquired the same level of education and academic prowess yet make different amounts of money. This is partly because their money-making skills and mentality are different.

Though you may both be doctoring the execution of the acquired knowledge and skills differ. One will wait to be formally employed. Another one will use the same knowledge, title, papers and set of skills to find other means of money-making (contracts with companies to offer health education; and screening health clients; open a clinic; locum shifts).

A friend of mine shared his story on WhatsApp on how he made himself marketable to have business and job opportunities. His name is Charles Lipenga: the co-founder of Maestros Leadership International. Initially, he tried to do what everyone else does: apply for jobs; wait for responses; find more applications. Yet this was to no avail. After several failed attempts, he grew in wisdom and went the unusual way. He offered to do a free internship at some company. They gave him a chance but couldn't give him proper tools (laptop) to work with. Imagine that! Working for them for free but couldn't even offer him the tools he needed to help them. Most people could have given up and walked away but he didn't.

But was it for nothing? Few months down the line people started appreciating his work. He built a CV and he started getting recognition and contracts from people and companies little by little. If you want someone to design a house for you, please don't hesitate to contact him, and you won't regret it. Right now, he is making money, just because he realized how to be patient, make a name whilst showcasing his work for free.

He had the very same knowledge which his classmates had who are probably still not employed right now.

He understood the process and the steps to take to get recognition and have a share of the market in architecture. It's not just about formal education when it comes to money-making but rather how educated you are at making money. Do you know how to make money, or you are just formally educated and feel entitled to have money?

Your papers don't work, they are nothing but tools. You sell your services to the employers and you must have skills to market yourself and deliver on the value promised. Aside from that, if you want to make more money then you have to increase your value through attaining new or rare skills and knowledge. Someone with a PhD is more likely to earn more money than one with only a first degree all things constant. If you want to be a top employee who earns more, increase in value and produce results.

Borrowing

People can earn temporary money through borrowing. These are people that sell ideas, stories and circumstances. Borrowing has its advantages and disadvantages depending on why and how we manage what we borrow.

For one to successfully borrow money from family, friends and even the bank, they need the knowledge and skill on how to do so. One relative asks for money, they get it, another goes and they don't. Sometimes is not favouritism from the giver rather the approach of the one asking.

Do you know who you are asking? Do you have leverage over them? I am not talking about blackmailing but what good do you have that would prompt someone to be willing to lend you their hard-earned money? What your behaviour like? You money track-record? Your business record? Your business plan and market research? Do you pay back debts as per agreement?

You need to have the knowledge and skills to check all the boxes that would increase your chances of borrowing money successfully.

One of the main reasons we end up borrowing or are still borrowing money is that we didn't know how best to manage the money we made in the past. The issue isn't how much we make against the needs we have, rather how what we make.

More especially for our generation, we are failing to

live our own lives. It's like we are competing to see who is more stupid when it comes to money mismanagement. Why can't you live comfortably in your own skin according to the level you are at now? Why squander the funds you were supposed to save and invest in the right things in line your purpose, mission and vision?

There is what is called good and bad debt. Good debt is only for those doing business or investment with a guarantee of having that investment payback on the loan. Don't be like our nation which gets money to eat not invest. If you want to borrow money, borrow not to start a business you are not familiar with, no matter how enthusiastic you are. I learnt this the hard way. You can borrow money if you want to expand on what you are already doing and is working.

Borrowing money is like borrowing seeds, you don't eat seeds, they belong in the garden where they bring you more, no matter how desperate you are.

This is an approach which you should take if you must borrow. Borrow money if and only if:

- you would want to invest in a business you already have an experience in, and you are sure that it will work out;
- you are investing but make sure you have at least 3 to 6 months before you start to give back the money.
- you have a sure way of giving back money like a salary, not someone who owes you money (I have been stupid several times from this but not

anymore). Don't count too much on your business to return the debt. Anything can happen;

- you have an emergency that needs money, and you can't have it any other way;
- you have money readily available somewhere to give back such as a faulty network that you can't access your money now;
- you have planned to give in instalments in a way that leaves you with enough money for basic needs for the other months so that you don't keep on borrowing.

Don't borrow money for interest unless all non-interest options have been exhausted and you need the money. Borrowing money often is not good for 2 things: 1. dents your reputation when you make a habit out of it and 2. you live like a slave without peace, more especially when you have a habit of not giving back. Life is meant to be enjoyed in peace.

Do whatever you can to build on your money-making skills and money multiplication skills. Don't wait till you retire to start these things, it will be too late for an old dog to learn new tricks. If you start now by the time you retire you will have picked a skill or two, some experience which will help you to start from somewhere after retirement if you still need to continue earning for sustenance. If you are good at it, you may even have a viable business which helps you retire early from your work as you employ people to help you with running your business. Remember no one leaves employment to their children unless they are a company owner.

Before you complain about not being employed, please look around you and find out the tools that you have which you can use for money-making including knowledge, skill, resources, etc. Educate your brain through knowledge and experiences to be able to see money-making opportunities even before they present themselves. Equip yourself to be ready to grab opportunities, build skills on how to open doors of opportunities.

Don't be a poor graduate, and lack of formal education doesn't mean you can't make money. Focus on learning money-making and handling skills and you can be as worthy as anyone can be. Napoleon Hill in his book "Think and Grow Rich" said that formal education only puts us on the path to real education (self-learning or self-centred learning) which includes money-making education. Formal education is meant to open our eyes on how to learn as we get into focused education that is tailored to our needs.

Money Handling Skills
"If your outgo exceeds your income, then your upkeep will be your downfall." – **Bill Earle**

Money is nothing but a resource or a tool. It is to be invested wisely just like time. So, how do you determine where to put your money if you don't know your purpose and vision?

After money has been made it needs to be managed.

There are two main reasons why people make money either to spend or create wealth. These goals are not met by how much money you make but rather how good you are at handling the "how much" you make. There are a lot of people who get deep in debt with more money they make.

After a year had passed, whilst doing my clinical internship, approximately MK3 million kwacha had passed through my fingers. I looked around for the tangible things I had done with it, I found none. I pretty much had the same clothes, same phone, same furniture; nothing new I could point at, yet all that money passed through my hands.

That was a wake-up call for me. I realized that there is something that I wasn't doing right. The fact that I was receiving it in bits doesn't justify why I couldn't still have something tangible to show. This is when I started putting efforts to invest in proper money management skills before it was another 10 years without anything to show for.

I am not the only one, I am just but a representation of many out there. I have heard a lot of people say this, and I know a lot of friends with the same experience.

If you want to live a happy and successful life in finances, you need to learn and put into practice the art of proper money management which has budgeting at the core of it. Yes, you read well, budgeting is the magic tool at the heart of money management. Without budgeting, you will have money and put it into unnecessary things.

If you can't manage to control the money that comes into your hands you will end up being poorer. How fast and how much you get rich is not dependent on how much you earn but rather on how much you keep and how good you are at money multiplication skills.

Money as A Tool

As said earlier, money is nothing but a tool or resource. Money is neither good nor bad, it's you who either get it or use it rightly or wrongly. If you make money your master, you'll get in trouble. Don't let money control you, you must decide how you get it and how you use it.

Look at money as a resource for your development and the world around you. It is nothing but a seed or potential to acquire anything that can be bought in life. That's why it is called a medium of exchange.
Every Tambala or penny to be spent must be budgeted and accounted for. Don't help people in a way that destabilizes your financial security even if it's relatives, unless it's an emergency and they can't get money any other way. You can't help others when you are drowning in financial debt.

Usually, we have plans to help our relatives acutely which usually have a bearing on our lives. Don't put too much on yourself, deal with what you can manage in a way that you can manage. They survived before you started making money and I don't think they would die now.

You should have a long-term plan to either equip them to make money or invest in something that will be making money for them. For example, saving part of the monthly money you would want to be giving them and buy them a minibus or a lorry that will be providing them money on a daily basis or open a shop for them which either they or you run for them.

For Africans, I know when we graduate usually a good chunk of our relative's financial burdens are placed upon our shoulders, but we need to be wise about it. When it comes to helping relatives through school, if there are a lot of them, then focus on those with potential that would provide returns from your investments. Don't help relatives the same, help in proportion to potential. Invest more in those with potential of being independent, those who will help you in helping the rest of your family. Don't let those with potential suffer in the name of helping everyone equally. Life isn't fair, and we need to be wise about it. It's not giving up on the other but making a wise investment.

Be wise, don't bring in emotions, because you might get overwhelmed and sink with them sooner or later. If being stingy for now is a good thing for the long-term then please do so without apology. It's the same principle of delayed gratification only that this time you are delaying other people's gratification for the greater good.

Budgeting

Budgeting gives you the power to channel your money even before it gets into your hands. Budgeting tells you in advance, before you have cash in your pocket, where, how much, when and why you should use the money. You know how much you need for what; how much to save, give to charity, you need for food, projects, airtime and the like. Without budgeting, you just realize you have spent your money on unnecessary things more especially when it feels like too much on the payday with no real plans beforehand. Make your budget and stick to it.

Budgeting works well when you know exactly where you need to put your money into. I don't just mean for business but school, personal development, ministry, family and friends, etc. Know your needs, where you should invest money into and when. You may have competing interests between things you need and want, assets and liabilities, etc but your purpose, vision and goals, and where you are in life should be the best judge of where to invest your money now. You may need to save for school in two years, a wedding or buying a car.

It's budgeting that tells you to be saving a certain amount to invest in something big that you can't afford at one go. It helps to know what you want to do with your income before it comes in.
Within budgeting, there are disciplines that you need to master such as saving and proper money allocation.

I am still learning more on budgeting and currently, my wife and I are enrolled in a life coaching program that touches on budgeting which has liberated our finances. Learn how to budget and track your money. It will help you even when you are a manager at your workplace when you start handling project money and budgeting for activities, and when in business. We need to handle life as a business.

Money Multiplication Skills

This is where things get tricky for those who have employment as their only tool in the box when it comes to money-making. They are limited to saving with their best options of money multiplication being a pension, investing in paper assets - bonds, policies and shares, and fixing their money for interest. They can't do businesses because they think it's risky and time-consuming. That's why it is challenging for people that depend solely on employment to be rich since they are limited in their money multiplication or making skills compared to those in business or investment.

There is usually exponential money growth in business when one runs it well, whilst employees wait upon salaries and allowances to save from.

As part of money management skills, whether you are working or not, you need to attain knowledge and skills in money multiplication through business and investment. Saving money is just as seed storage if the seed doesn't get destroyed by the weevils or natural disasters it remains as it is and to some extent devalues. The only way to multiply a seed is through planting it to bear more. After you save your money you should learn to plant it so that it can grow and bear more money.

If you just keep your money in the form of currency, it will lose its value through devaluation or inflation. You can't just keep your seeds with all the potential to grow into fruits and more seeds just because you lack the skills to do so. No one is born with skills, they are learnt.

Don't wait till you retire to give a shot at business or acquire business knowledge and skills. Start now little by little learning and doing business. By the time you are retiring you can do so comfortably knowing that you know other means of making money if you still need to make more money which is usually the case for most people.

God willing, if you get so good at money-making through business or investing you can choose to retire early from work and spend your time being your own boss, employing others, and spending time on your purpose and family. Everyone deserves to be happy in this life, but the power is in our hands to decide and pursue that.

Lending
Lending money to people should be done with the money that you wouldn't want back either soon or

ever. I know our sympathy usually betrays us but lending out money you will need soon, is a big mistake. You end up going around borrowing money yourself because someone didn't give you back in time. It's alright to have money that you have plans for and not lend it out when someone comes calling probably to use it in unprofitable things.

Look at the person you are lending to if you can trust them to give back your money. If possible, ask them when and how they are planning to return your money. It's your money, you have every right to ask the right questions to protect it.

I have owed people money for more months when I had promised to give back in a few days or weeks. I have also had people who did the same to me. If you can't lose it then don't lend it out. Lend money that you budgeted for charity or long-term saving if and only if you trust the person you are lending to.

RELATIONSHIP DEPARTMENT

Chapter Eighteen

For a purpose to be more effective, it must be done in relation to another entity whose function or purpose synergizes with it for a greater result or impact on the environment.

Remember that only independent people are the ones who are ready to get into interdependent relationships with others. If you are dependent in some areas, then in that area you are not ready to be interdependent with anyone. Yes, we should cover each other's weaknesses but not immaturity. Any kind of relationship or partnership whether romantic or not follows this principle or must follow this principle for effectiveness and sustenance.

Don't get into a romantic relationship if you don't know who you are, where you are going and if you are not emotionally, socially, mentally and spiritually independent or mature. Once again, maturity is not in age but rather in your ability to successfully run all the faculties of your life independent of the external influences. Being in a romantic relationship is a lot of work and I strongly discourage anyone who knows is not mature in some area to work on those areas first before getting into this venture.

Right Approach to Healthy Relationships

One of the reasons a lot of relationships die is that they are not healthy. Either one side or both don't benefit from it; there is more damage than benefit or just no benefit at all. Some people are usually in a relationship to benefit or take. They don't go in to help the other person but for them to be helped.

Relationship benefits are not just a matter of material things but also emotional and identity, among others. They depend on the other for their identity, fulfilment, happiness, meaning of life and sense of value. Whatever their partner or friends do sway their lives big time. These are the types of people that think their life is over just because someone broke up with them. They feel like they have lost everything, not because their partner was the best they could ever get in a lifetime or because they invested so much in them, but because they defined their lives through them. It's not loving with your all, it's just dependency.

I will repeat the statement that Steven R. Covey made in the 7 Habits of Highly Effective People, "Interdependence is a call that only independent people can make." Independent people are those that make things happen on their own and they have found their sense of worth. They

don't need anyone to determine how they feel or the self-image they have. What people say or do has little to no bearing on their lives. Such people are the ones that can take a step

further to connect and work with others. Independent people can spend hours by themselves without being bored, they can make themselves laugh and feel loved and appreciated.

When you have graduated from dependence to independence, then and only then can you take a step further into helping others feel comfortable in their skin. It's only at this level when you can offer opportunities to others and support them to do well in life without a tinge of jealousy. You have come to a place where you know that their success doesn't mean that you have failed or are failing which dependent people do. Independent people are like the X-axis on the graph whilst the dependent ones are like the Y that waits upon the X to act and they react. They live reactive lives. What differs are the kinds of reactions, some are linear, exponential, quadratic, etc.

As a human being, you need to make connections and have friends, and these should be more about giving and less of receiving, and no taking. Receive only when you have been given to, don't take; ask and receive when given to. This is key to success for any form of relationship whether romantic or not. What kills most friendships and relationships is the mentality of taking before you are given. Taking sex, emotions, peace, etc, this is what thieves and parasites do and no one would want to remain in contact with such.

One of the things that a lot of people miss out on when picking a relationship partner is the ability to see whether the person they want to approach or being approached by can give out or not. Healthy relationships will only work when two people that are willing to give more than they want to receive meet; people who make the relationship about the other's happiness and fulfilment. It's the same principle in a relationship with your spouse, family, community, society, nation and government. Be willing to give more than you are willing to receive. This is the only way a system or a society can be sustained.

Get this, if you want your relationship to work just like those you admire, go in to give. If you are already in one and not working, try to change the approach. Stop making it about you and what you want to get out of it and start making it about him or her. I am not saying you should compromise your values, standards and identity just to give in to the other person's demands or desires. If they are fine with you compromising on those things for their sake, it means they may like you, but surely, they don't love you. Those that love you value, respect and protect you, other than that it's not love but lust.

Someone gave a great illustration between love and like. He gave an example of a blossoming rose flower, those that love it water it to flourish and even blossom more whilst those that like it, pluck it off and probably give it to those they love. If you like something or someone you use them but if you love them, you either protect or provide to them the things you like to help them flourish and be happy.

Importance of Healthy Relationships

Having friends, connections and being in a relationship is like casting your net of opportunities wide. All these, work for your good just as you are there to work for their good.

If you know of an opportunity that fits a certain friend even if it can be a chance to get into a relationship with a seemingly better person than your partner, don't be jealous, notify them. Whether it is a job or school opportunity, even if they will be a competition, you don't know who will open a door for you tomorrow. Next time it's them telling you what you didn't have access to. That is life.

I remember the time I was writing my first 2 books, I talked to friends about them. Two of them connected me to people that would help with the editing, publishing and marketing of the books, and another led me to an author who could help me with selling and a target market I could sell to. All this information I didn't know about and probably I couldn't know if it weren't for friends.

The only reason we have been friends is that we give freely to each other without jealousy. We are there for each other when in need and we don't take from each other, we give, ask and then receive. Sometimes we receive even before we ask because we are also free to give without being asked to.

All forms of relationships are needed for most of us as far as purpose is concerned. For us to stand a chance to effectively achieve our purpose we will need to work hand-in-glove with others and the systems present. We might need to lead people or be under people to be built, and it all needs good relationship skills. Take it from me who has spent about 10 years under mentorship and about 4 years mentoring others, you need a good relationship and connection skills for you to get closer to your purpose.

The fact that you are at an independent level doesn't mean that you can do everything on your own. In the third book on this series, I will expand on productivity which has delegation and leverage at the core, which means you need good relationship skills for people to work with or for you one way or another. Even a good leader or an employer needs to have a good relationship with his or her subjects to keep them motivated and bring results. The goose that lays the golden eggs needs to be fed well and, in this case, having a good relationship with your subjects.

Even Jesus needed disciples and apostles to keep the vision going. Most of the great successful people needed their spouses to help them make their visions a reality. Most companies and organizations are successful because of employees or ground workers. Without good relationship skills, none of these people would be successful or at least wouldn't be as successful if they had to go at it solo. You need to synergize with other people with a common purpose for a greater effect.

I believe you are way better off in a healthy romantic relationship or marriage with a purpose because despite pursuing the common purpose, you have expanded income sources, more set of skills and brainpower, and you can be in several places simultaneously advancing that common purpose.

In a healthy marriage, you get to use one house, one bed and one car which is a lot of saving already. You get to cook for each other when the other can't, no need for maids. You don't have to be worried about unmet sexual desires because you are there for each other, meeting each other's needs. When your financial life is crumbling down, you relay on the other whilst sorting out your own. They are there to cheer you up in your low moments. This helps to bring stability in your lives compared to those that are single or in unhealthy relationships or marriages.

We need each other for support and greater good; the way an ecosystem, which humans are part of, should function - interdependent. You should learn to harness your meaningful relationships and connections if you want to go far. Learn and push to make a difference in their lives because they are the same people that will make a difference to you. There is an adage that says if you want to go fast go alone but if you want to go far then go together. In the end, life is about how far you go not how fast.

There is strength in numbers and indeed in a TEAM,

Together Everyone Achieves More than anyone would individually. By working together, you take advantage of each other's abilities. So, why go solo? Why be selfish?

AFTERWORD

I didn't write this book for fundraising, because if it was for fundraising, I would have priced it 5 to 10 times its current price. The wisdom in this book is priceless. I wrote this book as a solution to our decaying societies with quick fixes. I desired a functional system and a better environment around me by transforming your thinking through the enlightenment on purpose and interdependency.

As you read, the book is about building functional systems in homes, workplaces, among others, and for that to happen, it needs everyone to know who they are and what their roles and responsibilities are and take them up for the greater good.

If someone referred you to this book, it's because you are part of his or her system and they are trying to fix their system and environment too.

You are next in the chain, are you going to keep your environment at school, work, home and place of worship the same just because you don't want to share this information with others?

Remember you are better when those around you are

better! Stay blessed!

ACKNOWLEDGEMENT

I would like to thank God. This book has been birthed and wrought because of the progressive knowledge and keen desire to share what I believe has been on His heart. Grace has enabled me to be and grace will continually lead me home.

And to my amazing wife Sheena Khuwi who has demonstrated impeccable understanding as I have embarked on this endeavour that has steadily been on my heart. Thank you for being my first reader and helping with the initial editing as well. She is such a selfless woman who wants people to learn and be better. I would marry you again.

I would also like to thank my mentors (the Huwas - Cornelius and Jacqueline). The help you have both rendered all my life will forever be cherished. Dr C. Huwa - the reviews; the direction; the wisdom for this book. I am forever grateful. The chunk load that I have learnt from you has woven itself through the pages of this book. I can't thank God enough for you.

To Prof. Chiwoza Bandawe, a great friend and mentor, thank you for the wonderful foreword. I wouldn't think of any other person who could have better insight into this book than you. To Pastor Joseph Chikwenga, thank you for the guidance on the journey to publishing this book. Finally, to you, my readers, THANK YOU for choosing to read this book and learn from it.

ABOUT THE AUTHOR

Dr. Chilungamo Khuwi

Dr. Chilungamo Khuwi is a young Medical Doctor and a Christian who has spent a good time of his life teaching and mentoring people about purpose and living a balanced life.

He is a leader, and currently working with the International Training and Education Centre for Health (I-TECH) Malawi as a District Manager for one of their projects.

www.ingramcontent.com/pod-product-compliance
Lightning Source LLC
Chambersburg PA
CBHW071620150726
48000CB00004B/1813